UNITED NATIONS CONFERENCE ON TRADE AND DEVELOPMENT

Technical and statistical report

Gap Analysis of Cyberlaws in Pacific Small Island Developing States

United Nations
Geneva, 2025

United Nations Publications
405 East 42nd Street
New York, New York 10017
United States of America
Email: publications@un.org
Website: https://shop.un.org

This publication has been edited externally.

United Nations publication issued by United Nations Conference on Trade and Development

UNCTAD/DTL/ECDE/2024/6

ISBN: 978-92-1-003382-4
eISBN: 978-92-1-106996-9
Sales No. E.25.II.D.4

Acknowledgements

The Gap Analysis of Cyberlaws in Pacific Small Developing Islands States was prepared under the overall guidance of Torbjörn Fredriksson, Head, E-Commerce and Digital Economy Branch, Division on Technology and Logistics by a team comprised of Dan Svantesson (Consultant), Cécile Barayre, Chad Morris, Rodrigo Saavedra, Marcin Skrzypczyk, Thomas Van Giffen and Andrew Williamson. Contributions by Dominic Leong and Professor Ian Walden are also appreciated.

The publication greatly benefited from inputs from participants of UNCTAD TrainforTrade Blended Learning Course on the Legal Aspects of eCommerce, conducted from October to December 2023, as well as participants of the Workshop on Effective Legal Frameworks for Building the Digital Economy, jointly organized by the Pacific Islands Forum, the Commonwealth Secretariat, the Asian Development Bank and the United Nations Conference on Trade and Development, held in Suva, October 2023.

Comments and inputs provided by experts representing partner countries and the following eTrade for all partners and other international organizations have significantly enhanced the quality of the final report: the United Nations Capital Development Fund, the United Nations Commission on International Trade Law, the Commonwealth Secretariat, the Pacific Island Forum Secretariat and the World Bank.

The cover design was undertaken by the UNCTAD Communication and External Relations Section, and desktop publishing was carried out by Jesus Ales Villota. The report was edited by Romilly Sarah Golding. Administrative support was provided by Cynthia Faure and Diana Quiros.

UNCTAD extends its special thanks to Australia for its financial support provided in the preparation of this report. Financial support from other core donors to UNCTAD E-commerce and Digital Economy Programme is also greatly appreciated.

Abbreviations and acronyms

ADR	alternative dispute resolution
APEC	Asia–Pacific Economic Cooperation
ASEAN	Association of Southeast Asian Nations
B2B	business-to-business
ccTLD	Internet country code top-level domain
CCA	Commonwealth Connectivity Agenda
CERT	Computer Emergency Response Team
CIRT	Cyber Incident Response Team
C-PROC	Cybercrime Programme Office of the Council of Europe
CPTA	Framework Agreement on Facilitation of Cross-border Paperless Trade in Asia and the Pacific
CRA	Competition and Regulatory Authority
CSP	Cyber Safety Pasifika
DDS	digitally deliverable services
DNS	domain name system
EU	European Union
G20	The Group of Twenty
GDPR	General Data Protection Regulation
IANA	Internet Assigned Numbers Authority
ICPEN	International Consumer Protection and Enforcement Network
ICT	information and communications technology
IMF	International Monetary Fund
IP	intellectual property
IPEF	Indo-Pacific Economic Framework
ITU	International Telecommunications Union
LDCs	Least Developed Countries
MSMEs	micro-, small- and medium-sized enterprises
ODR	online dispute resolution
OECD	Organisation for Economic Co-operation and Development
PacCERT	Pacific Computer Emergency Response Team
PACERPlus	Pacific Agreement on Closer Economic Relations
PaCSON	Pacific Cyber Security Operational Network
PacLII	Pacific Islands Information Institute
PATCRA	The Agreement on Trade and Commercial Relations between the Government of Australia and the Government of Papua New Guinea

PICTA	Pacific Island Countries Trade Agreement
PIFS	Pacific Islands Forum Secretariat
PILON	Pacific Islands Law Officers' Network
PDEP	Pacific Digital Economy Programme
SIDS	Small Island Developing States
SPARTECA	South Pacific Regional Trade and Economic Cooperation Agreement
UNCITRAL	United Nations Commission on International Trade Law
UNCDF	United Nations Capital Development Fund
UNDP	United Nations Development Programme
WIPO	World Intellectual Property Organization

Foreword

Digital transformation is picking up pace in the Pacific, with technological advancements set to revolutionize onshore and offshore activities. The rise in connectivity, growing use of Information and Communication Technologies (ICT), and new digital innovations —some yet to reach the Pacific islands— are poised to unlock major economic opportunities, fuel rapid economic growth and create new jobs across the region.

However, realizing the full potential of e-commerce in Pacific Small Islands Developing States (SIDS), requires overcoming significant policy and legal challenges. To truly capture these "digital dividends", it is essential to create a supportive environment for the digital economy. This requires establishing comprehensive legal and regulatory frameworks that facilitate online transactions, ensure e-commerce security, and support the development of robust payment and transactional systems.

This Gap Analysis of Cyberlaws in the Pacific Small Island Developing State provides a timely analysis of the legislative developments in Pacific SIDS. It highlights significant gaps in cyberlaws across the region and reveals that no country has yet fully established comprehensive legal frameworks to support a thriving digital economy. Although some progress has been made, the absence of robust legislation continues to expose businesses and consumers to risks such as fraud, inadequate consumer protection and cybersecurity threats. These gaps not only hinder the growth of the digital economy but undermine the region's ability to fully engage in global online trade. However, the study shows that many countries are increasingly recognizing the weaknesses in their legal frameworks and are prioritizing reforms. Several countries are actively working toward adopting international and regional legal instruments, signalling a commitment to building stronger, more resilient digital economies.

By shedding light on these issues, this study serves as a vital resource for governments, stakeholders, and development partners, providing a roadmap to enhance legal structures and unlock new opportunities for sustainable digital growth in the Pacific. It calls for better coordination among development partners which is essential to ensure that assistance is effectively channelled towards building the necessary legal infrastructure and supporting the broader goals of digital transformation across the region.

This study is part of the Pacific Digital Economy Programme, a joint effort with the United Nations Capital Development Fund and the United Nations Development Programme. This initiative builds on long-standing assistance from UNCTAD to the Pacific Island Forum Secretariat and its members in support of the development of e-commerce, especially in the conduct of eTrade Readiness Assessments and E-commerce Strategies in the region.

I hope this analysis underscores the key legislative changes needed to build a strong digital economy in the Pacific, enabling the region to harness digital transformation for sustainable economic growth and better livelihoods.

Torbjörn Fredriksson
Head, E-commerce and Digital Economy Branch
Division on Technology and Logistics

Table of contents

Figures

Tables

Note

Within the UNCTAD Division on Technology and Logistics, the E-Commerce and Digital Economy Branch carries out policy-oriented analytical work on the development implications of information and communication technologies (ICTs), e-commerce and the digital economy. It is responsible for the preparation of the Digital Economy Report as well as thematic studies on ICT for Development.

The Branch promotes international dialogue on issues related to ICTs for development, and contributes to building developing countries' capacities to measure the digital economy and to design and implement relevant policies and legal frameworks. It also monitors the global status of e-commerce legislation (UNCTAD Cyberlaw Tracker). Since 2016, the Branch has coordinated a multi-stakeholder initiative entitled eTrade for all (etradeforall.org), which aims to improve the ability of developing countries, particularly least developed countries, to use and benefit from e-commerce. This initiative is also behind the UNCTAD eTrade for Women programme, launched in 2019, which aims to promote a more inclusive digital economy through its network of Advocates. These female digital entrepreneurs are active in all developing regions and contribute to capacity-building, mentoring and awareness-raising activities for more inclusive gender policies.

When the United Kingdom is mentioned, reference is made to the United Kingdom of Great Britain and Northern Ireland.

Reference to companies and their activities should not be construed as an endorsement by UNCTAD of those companies or their activities.

The following symbols may have been used in tables:

- **Two dots (..)** indicate that data are not available or are not separately reported. Rows in tables have been omitted in those cases where no data are available for any of the elements in the row.
- **A dash (—)** indicates that the item is equal to zero or its value is negligible.
- **Use of an en dash (–)** between dates representing years signifies the full period involved, including the beginning and end years.

The term "dollars" ($) refers to United States of America dollars, unless otherwise indicated. Details and percentages in tables do not necessarily add up to the totals because of rounding.

Part I

Cyberlaws in Pacific Small Island Developing States

A. Introduction

The Pacific region is witnessing a growing interest in digital transformation. Countries increasingly recognize the potential of e-commerce and digital trade to drive economic growth, enhance market access and improve livelihoods. However, several barriers remain, and addressing them requires collective effort. Hurdles include limited ICT uptake, restricted payment infrastructure and a shortage of digital skills. In many countries, establishing robust legal and regulatory frameworks is essential to fully enable digital transformation and ensure that digital activities can thrive sustainably across the region.

To address the need for a supportive legal and regulatory ecosystem, this study aims to provide a comprehensive analysis of the current legal landscape for e-commerce and digital trade in the jurisdictions of Cook Islands, Fiji, Kiribati, Marshall Islands, the Federated States of Micronesia, Nauru, Niue, Palau, Papua New Guinea, Samoa, Solomon Islands, Timor-Leste, Tonga, Tuvalu, and Vanuatu.

The study covers a range of topics, including electronic transactions and signatures, consumer protection, data protection and privacy, cybercrime and cybersecurity, intellectual property rights, online content regulation, domain names, online dispute resolution, digital identity, e-payments, and taxation.[1]

Within this study, "e-commerce laws" refer to the legal frameworks governing online transactions and digital business activities within a specific jurisdiction. These frameworks are typically designed to protect consumers and businesses operating in online markets within a country.

Cyberlaws have a broader international scope, covering cross-border trade of goods and services that involve digital elements. Cyberlaws include not only the movement of physical goods ordered online but also the transfer of data across borders, intellectual property rights in the digital environment, and international standards for cybersecurity and data protection. Cyberlaws facilitate trade by harmonizing regulations across countries, reducing trade barriers and ensuring consistency across digital standards. A definition of e-commerce and digital trade is provided in (figure 6).

Dedicated chapters for each country under review offer a detailed outlook of their specific e-commerce frameworks, assessing the progress made by individual countries and identifying gaps in current regulations. Through these country-specific analyses, the study aims to provide tailored insights that can guide policymakers, development partners and stakeholders in fostering a more robust digital economy in the Pacific.

1 This study focuses on indirect taxation of e-commerce and digital trade in Pacific Island countries.

B. Uptake of Information and Communications Technologies in Pacific Small Island Development States

Mobile broadband leads digital access in the Pacific, with 4G expansion outpacing fixed broadband growth.

It is beyond the scope of this study to examine all aspects of ICT development in the Pacific. However, recent developments driven largely by the deployment of submarine cables and satellite communications that have enhanced connectivity and Internet access– are helping to advance economic and regulatory environments in the region. This expanded infrastructure is essential for fostering e-commerce and digital trade and enables local businesses to reach wider markets and connect to global supply chains. Yet, persistent challenges such as high access costs, limited digital literacy and regulatory barriers continue to impede the region's full integration into the digital economy.

The Pacific region is witnessing varying levels of Internet connectivity across its nations, which presents challenges and opportunities for digital engagement. Across the region, mobile broadband subscriptions are growing at a faster pace than fixed broadband. With the expansion of 4G networks, mobile Internet is becoming the primary way that people connect online (figures 1 and 2).

Figure 1

Fixed broadband Internet subscriptions

(Per 100 people)

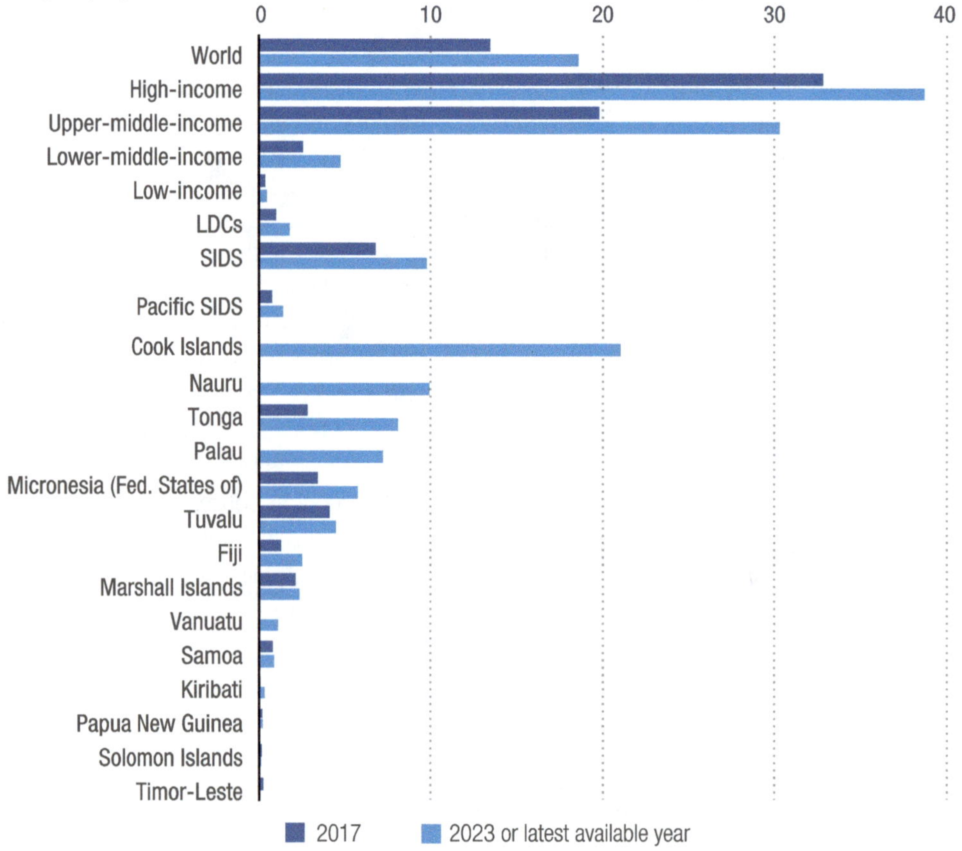

Figure 2

Mobile broadband Internet subscriptions

(Per 100 people)

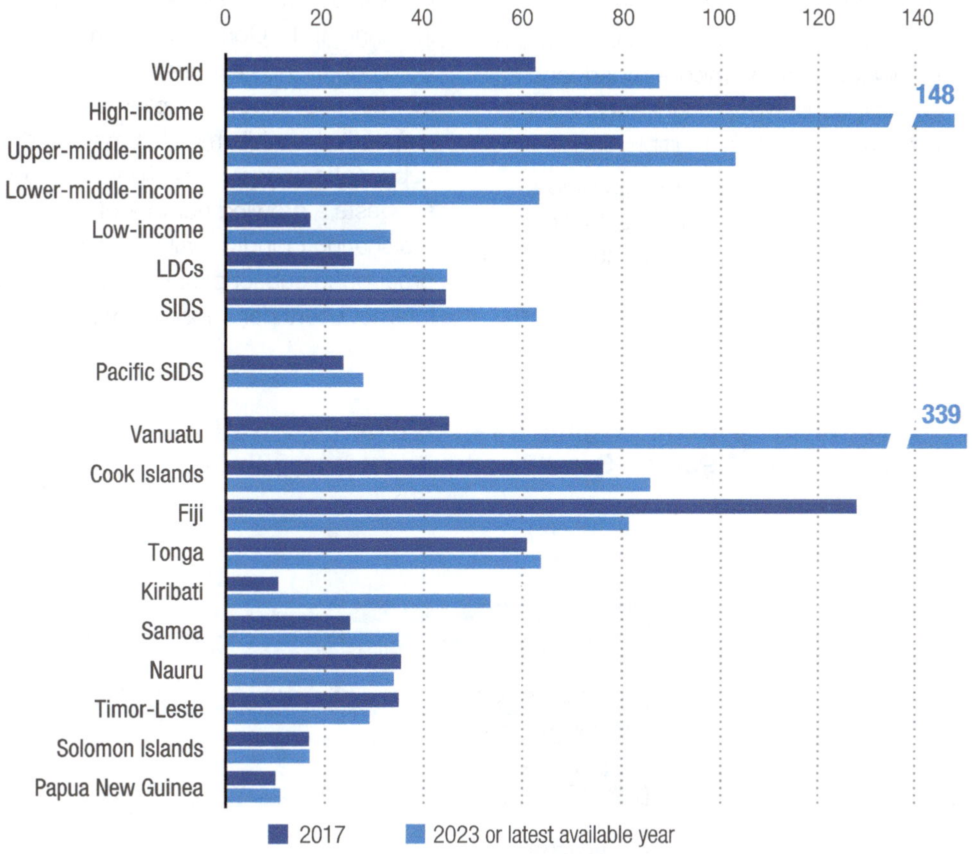

Source: UNCTAD calculations, based on International Telecommunications Union (ITU) statistics: Global and regional ICT data, updated November 2023, available at https://www.itu.int/en/ITU-D/Statistics/Pages/stat/default.aspx; and ITU DataHub, accessed 10/10/2024 at https://datahub.itu.int/query/.

Note: Where applicable, the latest data for 2023 concern Kiribati, Palau, and Timor-Leste and all country groupings (except Pacific SIDS); the data for 2022 concern other Pacific SIDS individually and Pacific SIDS as a group. If Papua New Guinea is excluded, which is the most populous country in the region, the Pacific SIDS average subscriptions would be: fixed-broadband Internet at 4 per 100 people and mobile-broadband Internet at 69 per 100 people. Figure 1: Vanuatu, Palau, Tonga, Nauru, Cook Islands data is not available 2017. Timor-Leste, Solomon Islands, Papua New Guinea data is not available 2023 or latest.

A comparison of mobile broadband subscriptions (figure 2) and Internet use (figure 3) across Pacific SIDS confirms the trend toward mobile Internet and highlights substantial progress from 2017 to 2023 or latest available year. This aligns with the broadband penetration targets from the Broadband Commission for Sustainable Development[2].

A snapshot of connectivity trends across the region:

- Fiji has among the highest access rates, with mobile broadband subscriptions at 81 per 100 people and Internet use at 85 per cent of the population, reflecting strong mobile connectivity reliance.

Connectivity across the region varies widely, with Fiji leading in access while other countries face persistent challenges.

2 https://www.broadbandcommission.org/advocacy-targets/3-universal-broadband/

- Papua New Guinea, Solomon Islands, Timor-Leste have the lowest connectivity rates, with low Internet use and low mobile broadband subscriptions.
- Nauru and Samoa have high Internet use combined with low mobile broadband subscriptions, which suggests shared subscriptions across multiple users.
- Vanuatu has exceptionally high mobile broadband subscription rates, likely driven by individuals holding multiple subscriptions for cheaper plans or network reliability.

Examining the evolution from 2017 to 2023 or latest available year, Kiribati and Vanuatu in particular saw both metrics more than double, signalling robust growth in connectivity. Conversely, Samoa and Solomon Islands experienced surges in Internet use –nearly doubling and tripling, respectively– while mobile broadband subscriptions grew only slightly. This trend suggests a growing number of individuals are sharing or individually using mobile broadband subscriptions, indicating a rise in Internet users per subscription.

Figure 3

Progress on broadband targets: Internet user penetration in select country groups and select Pacific Small Island Developing States

(Percentage of population)

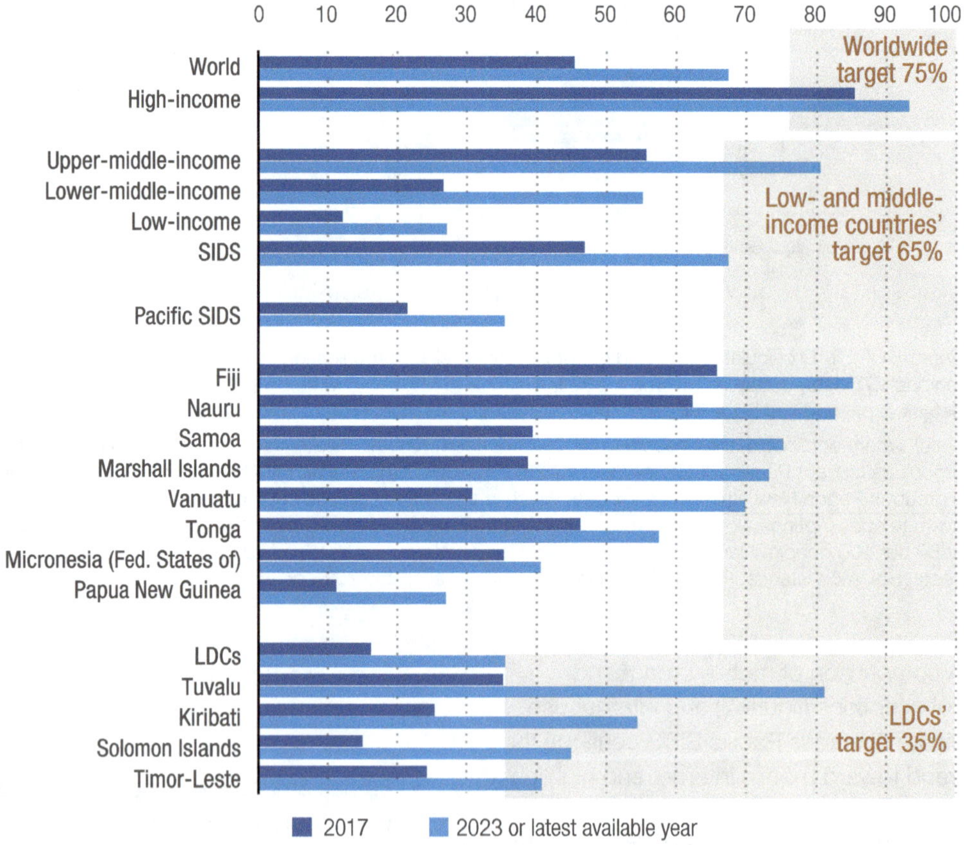

Source: UNCTAD calculations, based on ITU statistics: global and regional ICT data (update of November 2023), available at https://www.itu.int/en/ITU-D/Statistics/Pages/stat/default.aspx; and ITU DataHub, retrieved 10/10/2024 from https://datahub.itu.int/indicators/ Targets from Broadband Commission for Sustaibale Development for 2025 available at https://www.broadbandcommission.org/advocacy-targets/3-universal-broadband/ accessed on 21 January 2025.

Note: Latest available years are: 2023 (world and all groupings except Pacific SIDS); 2022 (Pacific SIDS as a group and all individual countries except Tonga); 2021 (Tonga). Country groupings are those of the source, except Pacific SIDS (UNCTAD).

Regional patterns in household Internet access:

- Countries such as Fiji and Nauru exhibit high levels of Internet access at home and robust individual usage (table 1), indicating strong overall connectivity.
- Kiribati and Papua New Guinea show higher household Internet access over individual use, likely due to factors such as affordability and limited digital literacy.
- In Tonga and Tuvalu, where Internet use is high but household access is lower, individuals may rely on mobile broadband or shared networks. This scenario underscores the critical role that mobile infrastructure and devices play in enhancing Internet connectivity throughout the region. The prominent role of mobile broadband or shared networks may also be influenced by pricing considerations.

Table 1
Core household digital access indicators, Pacific Small Island Developing States, 2022 or latest available year

	Percentage of households with access to computers and Internet				Percentage of population using Internet	
	Computer	Year	Internet access at home	Year	Internet	Year
Cook Islands	..	..	..	..	54.0	2016
Fiji	44.6	2017	79.9	2022	85.2	2022
Kiribati	31.4	2018	62.2	2022	54.4	2022
Marshall Islands	..	..	75.4	2022	73.2	2022
Micronesia (Fed. States of)	24.3	2017	31.4	2017	40.5	2022
Nauru	..	..	85.5	2022	82.7	2022
Niue	..	..	..	..	..	..
Palau	..	..	50.3	2017	..	..
Papua New Guinea	4.7	2017	29.3	2022	27.0	2022
Samoa	24.0	2017	77.1	2022	75.3	2022
Solomon Islands	7.3	2017	45.1	2022	45.0	2022
Timor-Leste	16.1	2017	18.2	2019	40.8	2022
Tonga	40.5	2017	33.8	2021	57.5	2021
Tuvalu	45.7	2017	67.4	2022	81.2	2022
Vanuatu	22.4	2017	69.3	2022	69.9	2022

Source: UNCTAD, based on ITU DataHub, retrieved on 10/10/2024 from https://datahub.itu.int/query/.

Note: The proportion of households with a computer or Internet access at home is calculated by dividing the number of in-scope households with a computer or Internet access by the total number of in-scope households. A computer refers to a desktop computer, a laptop (portable) computer or a tablet (or similar handheld computer). Internet access at home can be via a fixed or mobile network. Indicators for the percentage of the population using a computer and a mobile phone are not presented due to lack of available data for any country.

High smartphone use boosts e-commerce access, but limited tablets and computers may hinder full potential.

Internet connectivity is likely to improve across Pacific SIDS driven by more affordable connectivity options and improved availability to rural and underserved areas thanks to satellite communication. Given these developments, it is crucial to address the uneven access to digital infrastructure (as exemplified by the "Internet access at home" data in table 1) and devices in the region.

Recent surveys from the United Nations Capital Development Fund (UNCDF) provide valuable insights into digital device accessibility and usage (figure 4). According to 2022 data, smartphones are the predominant means of digital connectivity in the Pacific, with Tonga leading at 85 per cent, followed closely by Fiji, Vanuatu, and Samoa. Meanwhile, Timor-Leste and Papua New Guinea report moderate access levels, and Solomon Islands has the lowest rate at nearly 60 per cent. While high smartphone penetration is beneficial for increasing access to e-commerce, it may also limit user experience and functionality compared to greater access to tablets and computers, and potentially impact the overall growth and effectiveness of e-commerce in the region. Addressing these limitations through initiatives to promote more equitable access to diverse digital resources across populations is crucial for fostering a robust digital economy. One possible initiative includes setting up Internet kiosks or Internet cafes in rural areas, as these hubs can serve as access points for communities. Government support for access hubs like these can help lower the price for users.

Figure 4

Access to selected digital devices in Pacific Small Island Developing States, 2022

(Percentage of population)

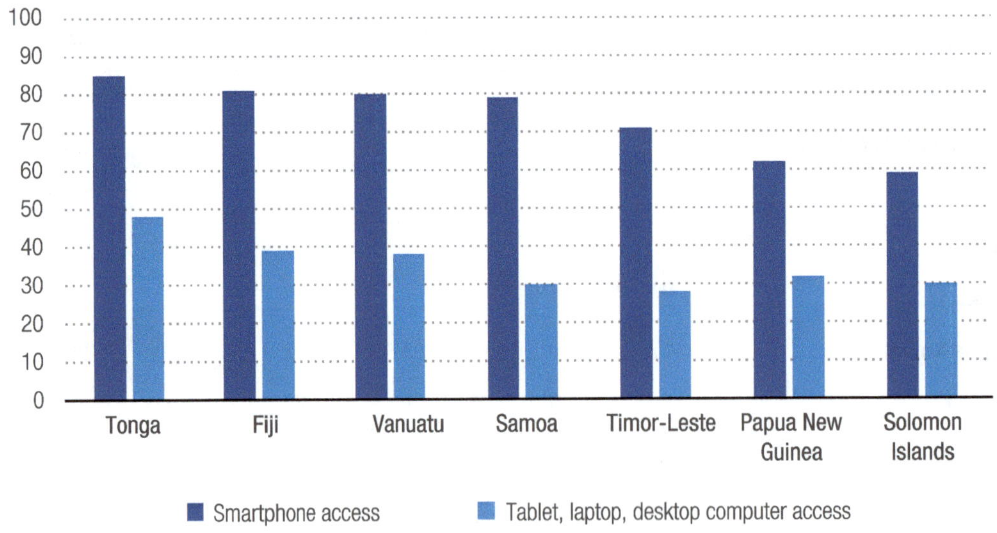

Source: UNCTAD, based on UNCDF survey reports (UNCDF, 2023a-g).

Furthermore, respondents to an export survey conducted by Pacific Trade Invest Australia in April 2024 highlighted three factors with a positive influence on online revenue generation for Pacific entrepreneurs. These are: easy access to digital devices such as smartphones, tablets, and laptops; increased customer usage of online channels; and improved ICT infrastructure, particularly in terms of Internet connectivity (figure 5).

Conversely, a country's legal framework (which includes consumer protection and cybersecurity) was not considered a priority. This lack of emphasis on the regulatory environment likely stems from a focus on the immediate needs that directly impact entrepreneurs' profitability, efficiency and growth. Additionally, there is a perception that the regulatory framework has limited relevance to daily business operations. This is further compounded by a general lack of awareness, limited interest and resource constraints. Bridging the gap between entrepreneurial priorities and the need for legal reforms is essential as neglecting these reforms could hinder entrepreneurs from enhancing their competitiveness and building consumer trust.

Figure 5

Factors driving online revenue generation among Pacific exporters

(Percentages represent the share of respondents within each group)

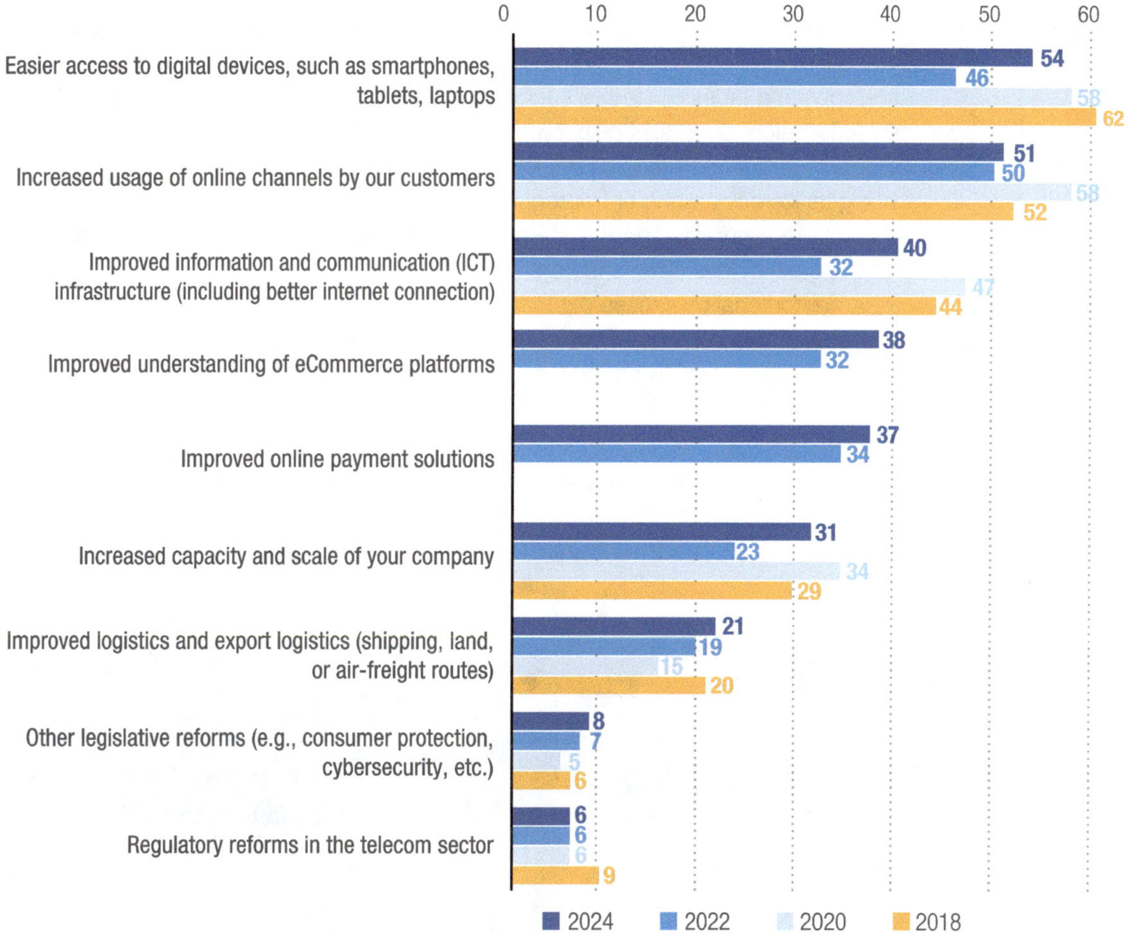

Source: Pacific Trade Invest Australia Export Survey 2024.

Note: The number of respondents (exporters generating revenue online) were as follows: in 2024 (192); 2022 (145); 2020 (168); and 2018 (133). The survey question (QE4) was: Please select the main factors that have positively impacted your ecommerce activities (i.e. generation of revenue online).

As ICT uptake continues to advance across the Pacific, smartphone penetration, improved ICT infrastructure and enhanced connectivity lay the groundwork for enhanced e-commerce and digital trade. The increasing reliance on mobile broadband further facilitates access to e-commerce platforms and digital marketplaces. This transformation can open new avenues for local businesses to engage in trade, diversify exports and broaden their markets. However, robust cyber laws are essential to support this progress and to ensure secure online transactions, to protect user data and foster trust in digital ecosystems.

C. Uptake of E-commerce and Digital Trade in Pacific Small Island Developing States

E-commerce and digital trade in the Pacific face unique challenges, yet hold potential for economic growth and resilience.

Countries in the Pacific grapple with limited digital infrastructure, moderate use of digital devices and the Internet, yet are also confronted with unique challenges and promising opportunities.[3] E-commerce and digital trade (figure 6) in the region is still in its early stages and faces obstacles such as geographic isolation, small and dispersed populations, high transportation costs, low levels of digital literacy among entrepreneurs, limited access to secure payment systems and high transaction fees. These factors make it harder for local businesses to participate fully in e-commerce. One particular challenge relates to economies of scale to export markets. Businesses that can only produce small quantities commonly incur high, or prohibitively high, shipping costs. There is also a need for supportive policies that foster a secure and inclusive digital trade environment. Additionally, promoting digital trade can drive diversification, economic growth and resilience. Since 2010, Pacific SIDS have experienced a persistent trade imbalance – particularly for goods. Imports such as fuel, machinery and manufactured products far exceed exports. There is a need to diversify through digital trade and expand digital exports to help offset a reliance on imports.

Figure 6

E-commerce and digital trade-fundamental concepts and definitions

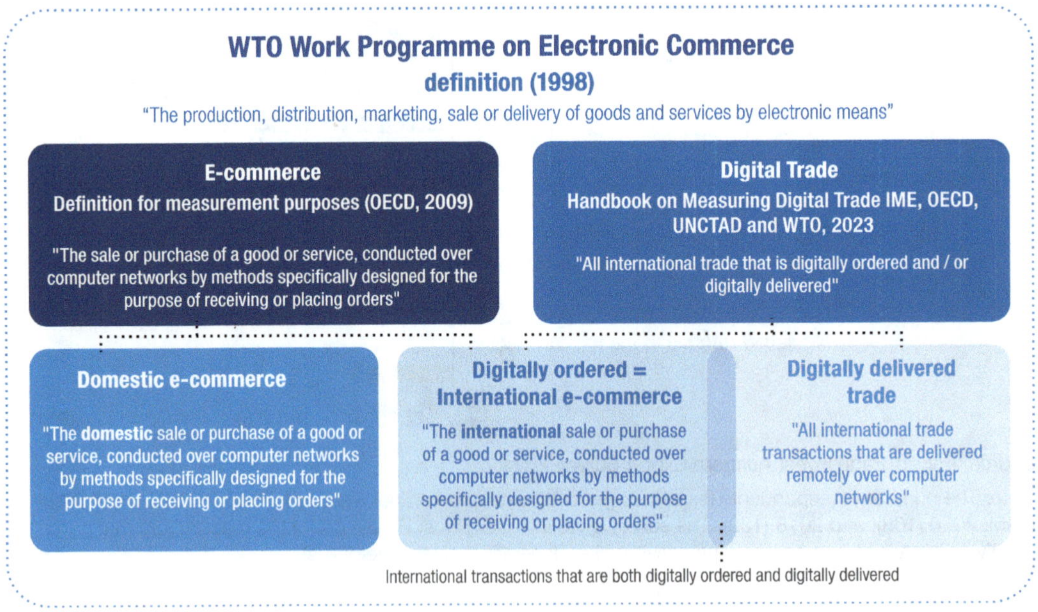

Source: IMF, OECD, UNCTAD and WTO.

Note: The statistical definitions of e-commerce and digital trade are fully compatible with the WTO definition of the Work Programme on Electronic Commerce. In addition to cross-border e-commerce, the WTO Work Programme also covers the domestic e-commerce activities of foreign owned or foreign-controlled service suppliers. The definition of digital trade given in this Handbook is also compatible with the description of e-commerce in IMF (2009) (i.e., "e-commerce is a method of ordering or delivering products at least partly by electronic means, such as through the internet or other computer mediated networks").

3 See *Pacific Digital Economy Report 2022* at: https://unctad.org/system/files/official-document/dtlecdc2022d4_en.pdf; and 2024 at https://unctad.org/system/files/official-document/dtlecdc2025d1_en.pdf.

In the services sector, trade has been volatile among Pacific SIDS, with tourism revenues contracting and recovering during the COVID-19 pandemic. This further highlights the potential for digital services to stabilize and boost trade across the region. Digitally deliverable services (DDS), while currently a minor component of overall trade and marked by a consistent trade deficit over the past decade, are a promising emerging area for economic diversification. They offer the potential to mitigate the constraints of geographic distance and reduce transportation costs tied to trade in goods or physically delivered services. Digitally deliverable services –which include software development, cloud computing, online education, telemedicine, digital media and online financial services– rely on digital networks to transfer electronic data remotely.[4] Strategic investment in DDS offers Pacific SIDS the potential to gradually build digital trade capabilities, encourage investment in stronger connectivity and improve access to essential digital services. While these efforts could contribute to a more diversified and resilient economy, realizing these benefits will mean overcoming challenges related to infrastructure, regulatory frameworks and skill development within the digital sector.

E-commerce in the Pacific region is progressively taking shape, supported by a range of initiatives and strategies designed to enhance digital trade. Pacific countries are actively working on this development, particularly through the Pacific E-commerce Initiative and the Pacific Regional E-commerce Strategy and Roadmap[5] which outlines a collaborative framework for implementing e-commerce initiatives. It also provides guidance on policy development, infrastructure improvement and capacity-building. Twelve countries have benefited from eTrade assessments,[6] while six have developed national e-commerce strategies (Cook Islands, Fiji, Samoa, Solomon Islands, Tonga, Vanuatu) and three are awaiting final Government approval before implementation (Papua New Guinea, Timor-Leste, Tuvalu). These efforts can strengthen e-commerce readiness, promote cross-border trade and enhance regional cooperation, boosting the digital economy in the Pacific.

While it is challenging to quantify the number of e-commerce transactions, two clear trends are emerging. First, small businesses are increasingly using social media platforms to promote their products and services to customers, reflecting the rise of informal commerce. However, these activities do not qualify as e-commerce transactions unless they involve automated purchasing processes specifically designed to receive or place orders.

Second, there is a rising trend of more formalized online shops and domestic retail platforms taking root in some Pacific SIDS. The entry of early-stage business-to-business (B2B) global retail platforms into the region signals a growing interest and potential for more structured e-commerce activities.

Together, these developments suggest that while e-commerce is still nascent, there is an emerging foundation upon which to build a digital trade ecosystem. As part of broader efforts to enhance digital transformation and support the growth of e-commerce in the region, banking institutions such as the Bank of South Pacific (BSP), the Australian bank ANZ, and the cooperative BRED Bank have introduced e-commerce business payment solutions for local businesses. This will make online transactions easier and smoother and enable online businesses to integrate end-to-end payments. These new steps are critical in a region where e-commerce growth has been constrained by a lack of digital payment infrastructure.

> Digitally deliverable services can diversify economies and reduce trade costs for Pacific SIDS.

> Addressing digital infrastructure and regulatory gaps is key to unlocking e-commerce potential in Pacific SIDS.

4 For more details about trade composition and trends in the Pacific, and the digitally deliverable services in particular, see UNCTAD *Digital Economy Report: Pacific Edition 2024* at https://unctad.org/system/files/official-document/dtlecdc2025d1_en.pdf.

5 See at: https://pacificecommerce.org/ and https://pacificecommerce.org/pei-project/regional-e-commerce-strategy-for-the-pacific/

6 Six eTrade Readiness Assessments were conducted by UNCTAD (Kiribati, Samoa, Solomon Islands, Timor-Leste, Tuvalu, Vanuatu) and six by the PIFS (the Federated States of Micronesia, Fiji, Nauru, Niue, Papua New Guinea, Tonga).

While this study focuses on national laws and regulations, international trade agreements also play an important role in facilitating cross-border e-commerce and harmonizing regulations across the region. Joining these agreements would be beneficial for Pacific SIDS, as they provide frameworks that can facilitate smoother trade processes, reduce barriers and improve market access for local businesses.

Currently, the involvement of Pacific SIDS in trade agreements is limited (table 2). Existing agreements contain few, if any, provisions that specifically address digital trade. A notable exception is the Indo–Pacific Economic Framework (IPEF), where Pillar I of the Framework emphasizes the importance of fostering an inclusive and resilient digital trade environment in the Indo–Pacific region.

Table 2
Bilateral and regional trade agreements involving Pacific Small Island Developing States and their digital provisions

Bilateral and regional trade agreements involving Pacific SIDS	Parties	Digital provisions
Agreement on Trade and Commercial Relations between the Government of Australia and the Government of Papua New Guinea (PATCRA)	Australia and Papua New Guinea	None
Interim Partnership Agreement between the European Community and the Pacific State	European Union (non-reciprocal tariff concession to eligible Pacific States)	None
Melanesian Spearhead Group (MSG) Agreement	Papua New Guinea, Solomon Islands, Vanuatu	None
Pacific Agreement on Closer Economic Relations (PACER) Plus	Australia, Cook Islands, Kiribati, Federated States of Micronesia, Nauru (not ratified), New Zealand, Niue, Palau, Marshall Islands, Samoa, Solomon Islands, Tonga, Tuvalu, Vanuatu	None
Pacific Island Countries Trade Agreement (PICTA)	Cook Islands, Kiribati, Marshall Islands, Federated States of Micronesia, Samoa, Tonga, Tuvalu, Vanuatu	None
South Pacific Regional Trade and Economic Cooperation Agreement (SPARTECA)	Australia and New Zealand (non-reciprocal tariff concession to Pacific Islands Forum countries)	None
Indo–Pacific Economic Framework (IPEF)	Australia, Brunei, Fiji, India, Indonesia, Japan, Malaysia, New Zealand, Philippines, Republic of Korea, Singapore, Thailand, United States, Viet Nam	None
Framework Agreement on Facilitation of Cross-border Paperless Trade in Asia and the Pacific (CPTA)	Armenia, Azerbaijan, Bangladesh, China, Iran (Islamic Republic of), Kyrgyzstan, Mongolia, the Philippines, Republic of Korea, Russian Federation, Tajikistan, Timor-Leste, Turkmenistan, Tuvalu, Uzbekistan	Pillar I emphasizes the importance of fostering an inclusive and resilient digital trade environment in the Indo-Pacific region

Source: UNCTAD.

By participating in such agreements, Pacific nations can align their regulations with international standards, enhance cooperation with trading partners and create a more predictable and secure environment for digital transactions to drive economic growth and resilience in the digital economy.

To address the challenges and seize the opportunities of e-commerce and digital trade in the Pacific, comprehensive cyber law reforms and a well-structured legal framework are essential. Reforms can provide the foundation for secure online transactions, build trust in digital platforms and support inclusive and resilient digital trade ecosystems. By aligning legal frameworks with international standards and best practices, Pacific SIDS can create a more enabling environment for businesses to overcome barriers, diversify their exports and fully participate in the global digital economy.

D. Overview of the Status of Cyberlaws in the Pacific

No country in the region has established a comprehensive legal framework for e-commerce. Progress varies significantly across countries (table 3) with many Pacific SIDS facing significant challenges in modernizing their legal systems due to limited resources and technical expertise. This has resulted in a fragmented legal landscape where e-commerce-related regulations are either absent, incomplete or not uniformly enforced. A few countries are advancing e-commerce and policy frameworks to enhance digital trade and economic resilience. For example, Timor-Leste is moving ahead with its legal framework for e-commerce through the recent enactment of Decree-Law No. 12/2024, which introduces regulations for electronic transactions, digital signatures and e-commerce. Many countries in the region have or are in the process of developing e-commerce strategies and policies that address consumer protection, data privacy, intellectual property rights and competition. Collectively, these efforts aim to foster economic growth, increase participation in global value chains, and enhance opportunities for micro-, small-, and medium-sized enterprises (MSMEs) in these island nations. These measures are often supported by partnerships with regional bodies and international organizations, including UNCTAD and the Pacific Islands Forum Secretariat.

Cybercrime, cybersecurity, e-transactions and e-signatures are among the areas of law that have the most comprehensive legislative coverage in the region. In these fields, many jurisdictions have established laws and regulations to address the complexities of the digital environment. However, other areas, such as intellectual property and copyright, often lack the necessary adaptations to address cyber-specific challenges, despite a significant number of countries having foundational laws in place.

Online content regulation, consumer protection and taxation are generally governed by technology-neutral laws, which often fall short in addressing cyber-specific issues.

Progress has been slower in other areas, such as domain names, e-payments and digital identity. While some countries have established legislation in these fields, others are still in the drafting stages. Data protection and privacy laws remain particularly underdeveloped, with no comprehensive legislation currently in place, although some countries are working on draft laws. Significant gaps also exist in areas such as online dispute resolution, where robust legal frameworks have yet to be established. This highlights the pressing need for more comprehensive regulations to support the growth of digital trade in the region.

Addressing these gaps is essential for fostering digital trade in the region. Without a solid legal framework, economic development is likely to be stifled, and Pacific countries may struggle to fully participate in the global digital economy.

The remainder of this section provides a detailed overview of the state of play in Pacific SIDS for each area of focus in this study.

1. Electronic transactions and electronic signatures

E-transaction laws are vital in digital trade because they provide the legal foundation needed to ensure trust, security and efficiency in online transactions. They address key areas such as validating electronic communications, regulating electronic payments and the use of digital signatures. Digital signatures, which authenticate and secure electronic interactions, often rely on trusted third-party intermediaries. By covering these aspects, e-transaction laws enable secure and reliable digital transactions which are essential for both domestic and international trade.

Harmonizing e-transaction laws enhances legal consistency, boosting e-commerce growth across jurisdictions.

Of the studied jurisdictions, Fiji, Kiribati, Papua New Guinea, Samoa, Timor-Leste, and Vanuatu have all adopted specific legislation on e-transactions based on models from the United Nations Commission on International Trade Law (UNCITRAL). Fiji, Kiribati, Papua New Guinea, and Timor-Leste have also adopted e-signature provisions based on UNCITRAL models. In Fiji, the Electronic Transactions Act 2008, and subsequent amendments in 2016 and 2017, brought national legislation in line with the United Nations Convention on the Use of Electronic Communications in International Contracts (2005) (the "Electronic Communications Convention"). Kiribati and Tuvalu acceded to the Electronic Communications Convention in 2022; the Convention entered into force in Kiribati in 2020 and in Tuvalu in 2023. The Electronic Transactions Act 2021 in Papua New Guinea provides a legal framework for online transactions and, importantly, legitimizes a framework for electronic signatures. The Act incorporates the UNCITRAL Model Law on Electronic Transferable Records (2017) which supplements the 2005 Convention. Kiribati has also adopted the UNCITRAL Model Law on Electronic Transferable Records (2017). Timor-Leste adopted Decree-Law No. 12/2024, based on the UNCITRAL framework, to regulate digital interactions and e-commerce, enhance digital interactions and validate electronic records and signatures. In Vanuatu, the Electronic Transactions Act 2000 generally follows the UNCITRAL Model Law on Electronic Commerce.

Regulatory frameworks in the Pacific are often outdated and inconsistent, creating gaps in online consumer protection.

2. Online consumer protection

Consumer protection laws are essential to digital trade because they ensure fairness, transparency, and security for consumers engaging in online transactions. These laws safeguard consumers from fraud, misleading practices and breaches of privacy while generating trust in e-commerce platforms. By providing legal recourse for disputes, regulating product standards and ensuring data protection, consumer protection laws create a reliable environment for digital trade, encouraging consumer confidence and promoting market growth both domestically and internationally.

None of the studied jurisdictions have specific laws for consumer protection in e-commerce. This pattern is also observed globally. The merit of adopting a technology-agnostic consumer protection law that covers both digital and offline transactions lies in its ability to eliminate the need to define which transactions fall under e-commerce and which do not. Nevertheless, even in cases where a country chooses a technology-neutral approach, there is a need to explicitly state that the consumer protection law is equally applicable to e-commerce activities.

Although existing consumer law protections in a few Pacific jurisdictions apply to online transactions, there remains some uncertainty about their scope, applicability and enforcement. In the majority of jurisdictions, consumer protection is predominantly provided via a patchwork of partially overlapping legislation. This is the case in Cook Islands, Papua New Guinea, and Samoa. Nauru adopted a comprehensive consumer protection law, the Consumer Protection Act 2023. Significant gaps exist in the degree of online consumer protection provided in the region; regulatory frameworks are generally outdated and inconsistent and many do not address consumer rights and recourse within digital markets.

3. Data protection and privacy

The growing significance of personal data in digital trade has raised concerns about safeguarding consumer information. Consumers want to be assured that their personal data will be protected when engaging in transactions. At the same time, the substantial benefits derived from data flows in trade and digital commerce highlight potential constraints to business operations as a result of stricter privacy regulations. Digital activities are heavily reliant on data, and safeguarding data is crucial for the success of the digital economy and to attract investors. Clear, consistent and robust data privacy regulations will inspire trust in consumers and businesses alike. The main aim of data protection legislation is to safeguard individuals against the misuse of personal information, whether it identifies them directly or indirectly.

None of the jurisdictions studied have adopted comprehensive laws or regulations on data protection and privacy. Some countries are making headway – Timor-Leste has developed a draft Data Privacy and Protection Law and Vanuatu introduced a draft Bill for the Data Protection and Privacy Act in 2024, which aims to protect personal data in line with international standards. The absence of data protection and privacy laws can have significant economic repercussions. Without a legal framework to safeguard personal information, consumers may be hesitant to engage in digital transactions, fearing that their data could be misused or compromised. This lack of trust can hinder the growth of e-commerce and digital trade, limiting market expansion and innovation. Businesses may also face increased risks of data breaches and the resulting reputational damage, leading to potential financial losses. Jurisdictions without robust data protection measures may struggle to attract foreign investment, as international companies often seek environments that prioritize data security and consumer privacy. The absence of comprehensive data privacy laws can hinder online businesses from accessing larger global markets –such as the European Union– due to stricter data privacy requirements.

Additionally, none of the countries in this study have a unified, whole-of-government approach to data privacy and protection. This absence of coordination increases the risk of fragmented, inconsistent practices, leading to non-harmonized requirements for data use and the lack of a cohesive national policy framework.

The Pacific jurisdictions are working on developing modern data privacy laws. However, it is uncertain whether adopting highly complex data privacy frameworks, like those seen globally, is the most effective approach for these regions. Further efforts are needed to identify the core components of data privacy laws that can provide meaningful protection, particularly for the smaller economies and developing countries included in this study. Data privacy legislation must be accompanied by appropriate structures. One option is to build on existing experiences with an ombudsman – several of the jurisdictions studied have an ombudsman in place and experience with working with this structure (see e.g., the Samoa Ombudsman (Komesina o Sulufaiga) Act 2013, the Ombudsman Act of Tonga (Cap. 2.02), and the Ombudsman of Solomon Islands (Further Provisions) Act (Cap. 88)).

> The lack of data protection laws stifles e-commerce growth and erodes consumer trust.

Attention could also be directed to matters such as whether to adopt special data privacy protection for children, as in the Marshall Islands' Child Rights Protection Act 2015.

Apart from introducing comprehensive and dedicated data privacy legislation, the Pacific jurisdiction may consider the role of civil non-contractual actions. In some of the examined jurisdictions, evidence of a tort for privacy violations was found.

4. Cybercrime and cybersecurity

Cybercrime refers to criminal activities conducted through networks, technological devices and the Internet. Laws related to cybercrime empower authorities to take action against such violations. While interpretations of cybercrime vary by country and legal context, all nations require legislation that targets criminal behaviour. This includes actions that undermine the confidentiality, integrity and accessibility of computer systems, networks and the data they hold, as well as offences executed using these technologies.

Dedicated cybercrime laws across the Pacific enhance e-commerce safety by addressing a range of cyber offenses.

A number of Pacific jurisdictions have enacted dedicated cybercrime legislation or incorporated cyber offences into their criminal statutes. The criminal laws, whether articulated through dedicated cybercrime statutes or technology-neutral legislative frameworks, address a wide range of issues ranging from cyberbullying to the integrity and availability of computer data, as well as other computer-related and content-related offences. Noteworthy instances include provisions found in Part 8 of the Nauru Crimes Act 2016 and in Tonga, the Electronic Communication Abuse Offences Act 2020. In the latter, specific measures have been instituted to address these concerns. Regional and international developments have also taken shape, with Tonga having acceded to the Convention on Cybercrime of the Council of Europe (Budapest Convention). Meanwhile, Fiji, Kiribati, Timor-Leste, and Vanuatu are recognized as observer countries to the Budapest Convention.[7]

The Cook Islands, Guam, Kiribati, Nauru, Niue, Palau, Papua New Guinea, the Marshall Islands, the Federated States of Micronesia, Samoa, Solomon Islands, Tonga, Tuvalu, and Vanuatu actively participate in the "Cyber Safety Pasifika" (CSP) programme facilitated by the Australian Federal Police. This initiative is designed to enhance awareness and education on cyber safety within vulnerable communities across the Pacific region. The programme also includes a focus on training and capacity-building for Pacific police officers in the field of cybercrime investigations.[8] All jurisdictions within the study are members of the Pacific Islands Law Officers' Network (PILON). This network addresses key law and justice issues and contributes to fostering a safe and secure Pacific region.[9] Importantly, the PILON network includes a specific Cybercrime Working Group.[10]

Cybersecurity frameworks provide legal provisions to identify critical national infrastructure and data. Typically, cybersecurity measures establish the necessary organizational and technical security principles, enforce transparency obligations, ensure adherence to standards and define oversight and enforcement mechanisms.

Cybersecurity is a rapidly growing threat globally. Recent cyberattacks in several Pacific countries, including Palau, Papua New Guinea, Samoa, Tonga, and Vanuatu have highlighted significant vulnerabilities in the region's cybersecurity infrastructure. There is an urgent need for regional cooperation and support from international partners to enhance security and resilience against such threats. In response, initiatives like the Pacific Cyber Security Operational Network (PaCSON) and national strategies such as the National Cyber Security Strategy in Vanuatu, have been developed to address cybersecurity threats.[11]

Several jurisdictions have made progress in developing distinct cybersecurity frameworks. Papua New Guinea has a

7 https://www.coe.int/en/web/cybercrime/parties-observers.
8 https://www.cybersafetypasifika.org/our-work/about-cyber-safety-pasifika.
9 https://pilonsec.org/about/members/.
10 https://pilonsec.org/our-work/working-groups/cybercrime/.
11 https://forumsec.org/publications/pacific-security-outlook-report-2022-2023

National Cyber Security Policy (2021) aimed at protecting critical infrastructure, while Fiji is developing a National Cybersecurity Strategy alongside its existing cybercrime laws. The Vanuatu Cybercrime Act 2021 includes cybersecurity provisions, and Nauru has integrated cybersecurity aspects into its Communications and Broadcasting Act 2018. In Tonga, the Computer Emergency Response Team (CERT) is operational, and a dedicated Cybersecurity Bill is under consideration. These efforts highlight the region's increasing focus on cybersecurity as a critical component for safeguarding its digital infrastructure and activities.

5. Intellectual property and copyright

Intellectual property (IP) laws, which include copyright, patents, trademarks and other forms of protection, are crucial to digital trade. IP laws, which involve multiple legal considerations, help protect innovations, creative works and brands, while encouraging local entrepreneurs and businesses to invest in new ideas. This protection fosters economic growth, development and investments, particularly in the creative industries, agriculture, tourism, and the technology sector, all of which are highly relevant in the Pacific. Additionally, IP laws can help protect traditional knowledge, cultural expressions and Indigenous rights. This is especially important in the Pacific, where many communities have rich cultural heritages that need safeguarding from exploitation and misappropriation. Indeed, some Pacific countries, such as Niue, make specific provisions within their IP laws to protect traditional knowledge and expressions of culture. Strong IP laws facilitate trade by ensuring that products and services meet international standards. This is crucial for Pacific countries looking to participate in global markets, as it allows them to leverage their unique products and cultural assets effectively.

IP laws in the Pacific are governed by a variety of local regimes, reflecting a blend of historical influences and modern legislation. International agreements heavily influence IP and copyright regulations, with nearly all jurisdictions having relevant legislation, generally drafted in a technology-neutral manner. For example, in Tonga, the Copyright Act (Cap. 17.05) includes technology-neutral and technology-specific provisions relevant to e-commerce, such as Section 14 on the reproduction and adaptation of computer programs. In some instances, such as in Papua New Guinea, intellectual property is addressed in cybercrime legislation. The Cybercrime Code Act 2016 includes provisions for intellectual property offences, specifically online copyright, trademark and patent infringement. Recent legislative updates in the region include Law No. 14/2022, dated December 22, which introduced a comprehensive regulation of intellectual property and copyright in Timor-Leste. Major law reforms were gazetted in 2021 in Fiji, encompassing the Designs Act 2021, the Patents Act 2021 and the Trademarks Act 2021. Most jurisdictions are members of the World Intellectual Property Organization (WIPO) and are signatories to the Berne Convention for the Protection of Literary and Artistic Works.

> Cybersecurity vulnerabilities in the Pacific threaten e-commerce growth, highlighting the need for regional cooperation.

6. Online content regulation

Content regulation includes blocking, limiting or removing content that has been made available online, as well as restricting access to objectionable material, licensing arrangements and user account suspensions. However, there is no universally accepted definition of this term, and it intersects with issues like the roles of social platforms, freedom of expression and the types of content involved. Given that Internet companies manage vast amounts of personal data, regulation impacts privacy, free expression and public engagement. Government policies and user agreements dictate content moderation, with liability protections for intermediaries often leading to ambiguous restrictions. The global trend

> Effective content regulation is essential for e-commerce, fostering trust and ensuring safe digital trade environments.

towards monitoring user-generated content poses compliance challenges and involves diverse legal frameworks. While moderation standards through terms of service are common, vague definitions around prohibited activities can result in inconsistent enforcement and bias, highlighting the complexities of content regulation and the need for careful formulation and enforcement.

Online content regulation is vital for digital trade in the Pacific, as it creates a safe and trustworthy online environment for businesses and consumers. Effective regulation curbs the spread of harmful or illegal content, such as fraud, mis- and dis-information, and intellectual property theft, which can erode consumer confidence and hinder economic growth. By enforcing quality and safety standards, these regulations facilitate smoother cross-border transactions and protect local businesses from unfair competition while promoting local cultures and content.

Few countries effectively govern domain names, impacting e-commerce and digital trade security.

The regulation of online content in the examined jurisdictions typically stems from constitutional provisions acknowledging the freedom of expression. This freedom of expression is, when necessary, weighed against other constitutional rights like privacy and the right to reputation. In addition to constitutional provisions, content regulation primarily revolves around limiting specific content types, usually through local laws that apply regardless of the technology used. However, there are instances of technology-specific content legislation explicitly addressing the online environment, such as the Online Safety Act 2018 in Fiji and, in Tonga, the Electronic Communication Abuse Offences Act 2020. Certain content-related provisions are drafted in technology-specific language which can hinder the effective application of laws in the online environment. For instance, the Penal Code of Solomon Islands specifically mentions the "Prosecution of obscene video tape or photograph" (Section 174).

Finally on this topic, in certain jurisdictions, the regulation of online content is guided by a national broadcast policy or code.

7. Domain names

A domain name is a text-based address that corresponds to one or more numeric IP addresses and is used to identify specific web pages on the Internet. As such, a domain name functions as an "address" used to refer to a specific location on the Internet or to an email address. The Internet relies on a foundational layer known as its "logical infrastructure" – the systems and rules, like Domain Name Systems (DNS) and IP addresses, which are essential for managing and routing data online. The Domain Name System (DNS) is a crucial element in the logical infrastructure supporting communication networks and the Internet. The growing interest of policymakers in DNS and its security stems from an increased awareness of its critical role. As a foundational part of the Internet's logical infrastructure, digital security incidents affecting DNS availability, integrity or confidentiality can have significant societal impacts. Indeed, the DNS is considered to be a national resource that should be appropriately managed. It is therefore integral to establish the requisite oversight body through legislation.

The governance of domain names (including the country code top-level domain or "ccTLD") often falls under telecommunications legislation. For example, in the Cook Islands, Part 7 of the Telecommunications Act 2019 regulates domain administration for the ".ck" top level domain. Likewise, Section 30B(1)(b) of the Communications Act 1989 states that "the ccTLD .nu is a National resource for which the prime authority is the Government of Niue." In Papua New Guinea, the Digital Government Act 2022 outlines specific rules regarding the Government domain, including the responsibilities of Governmental departments in administering domain names.

8. Online dispute resolution

Online dispute resolution (ODR) encompasses technology-driven methods such as arbitration and mediation for resolving disputes without litigation, especially e-disputes. It includes online settlement via expert systems (computer programmes that simulate decision-making), arbitration with qualified arbitrators, and mediation with qualified mediators. Particularly promising in regions lacking physical infrastructure, ODR has the potential to enhance consumer trust and support e-commerce growth. ODR modernizes justice systems, improves access to justice, and addresses legal needs for individuals, businesses, and communities. However, traditional alternative dispute resolution methods face credibility issues due to impartiality concerns and low enforceability. To address this, improving digital skills among justice civil servants, diversifying the appeal of alternative dispute resolution and promoting awareness of dispute resolution options are crucial.

None of the studied jurisdictions have legislation specifically addressing ODR. One possible starting point for further work in this area can be found in the existing small claims tribunals, such as those in Fiji and Tuvalu. These tribunals could be expanded and tailored for online dispute resolution. Additional institutional developments may also provide a foundation for establishing ODR, such as creating a governing body for mediation in Samoa and, in Papua New Guinea, drawing inspiration from national rules on alternative dispute resolution following the implementation of the Arbitration (International) Act 2024.

9. Digital identity

Digital identity refers to the unique set of information and attributes associated with an individual, organization, or object that is used to identify them in the digital world. Digital identities encompasses data such as usernames, passwords, biometric data (fingerprints, facial recognition), digital certificates and any other personal or object identifiers (e.g., email addresses, social media profiles, digital object identifiers (DOI), etc) that are used to authenticate or validate an entity's presence and activities online. Digital identities are used to access services, conduct transactions and participate in various online activities. They play a critical role in ensuring security, privacy and user authentication in digital interactions. However, they also present challenges related to identity theft, privacy protection and verification.

Great care must be taken to ensure that digital ID structures do not create new inequalities or exacerbate existing ones. In any jurisdiction with restricted connectivity, low Internet usage, or limited digital literacy, digital ID structures risk creating or exacerbating discrimination. Ensuring connectivity for all and achieving sufficiently high levels of digital literacy are essential prerequisites for implementing digital ID structures. Furthermore, where adopted, digital ID structures become integral and sensitive features of society. As such, they must be conceived, structured, implemented and regulated with resilience in mind.

The Pacific has experienced a rise in the deployment and use of digital technologies, along with efforts to establish and enhance national identification and registration systems. Pacific Island countries are progressively restructuring their legislative systems to address the demand for effective service delivery to their citizens. This includes ensuring the security and sustainability of various Government programmes and initiatives.

For example, the Digital Government Act 2022 of Papua New Guinea establishes digital governance by leveraging ICTs. It focuses on the planning, coordination, development and implementation of digital services, infrastructure, skills and other aspects of digital governance across all Government sectors.

> Without legislation for ODR, e-commerce struggles as consumer trust and dispute resolution options remain limited.

> The lack of digital identity legislation challenges the security of e-commerce transactions.

The Papua New Guinea Government Digital Identification Standards and Guidelines 2023, issued under Section 64 of the Digital Government Act 2022 prescribes standards and guidelines for Government digital identification. This instrument seeks to create a secure, user-friendly digital identity ecosystem, improve online security, simplify identity management and empower individuals. Additionally, it supports public bodies in confidently engaging in digital transactions and accessing digital services while ensuring privacy and trust are maintained.

The Samoa National Digital Identification Bill 2023 aims to establish a national digital identification system that safeguards personal data. The Bill's objectives are to: (a) implement a modern digital identification system for registering citizens and residents of Samoa; (b) create a digital, unique, and legally recognized identity for each registered individual; and (c) provide a means of authenticating registered individuals, and protect their personal data.

Expanding e-payment systems are vital for e-commerce growth, yet regulations in the Pacific are lagging.

10. E-payments

E-payment systems are experiencing significant global expansion, creating new opportunities for consumers and businesses in e-commerce. Key policy and regulatory initiatives focused on enhancing efficiency are actively shaping the landscape of payment services. Regulators are stepping in to improve the efficiency of payment services, addressing the slow adaptation of traditional providers while fostering collaboration with emerging payment solutions. Policy-driven efficiency, regulatory reforms, data control and interoperability are crucial in advancing e-payment systems and significantly enhance the growth and success of e-commerce.

Digital payment-related regulations in the Pacific are generally not reflective of the ongoing developments in the digital payment space. However, several countries have developed or are in the process of developing legislation that encompasses digital payments and electronic money. For instance, the Papua New Guinea Digital Government Act 2022 contains provisions relating to e-payment (see e.g., Section. 35(2)(e)(iv)) and the Fiji National Payment System Act 2021 empowers the Reserve Bank of Fiji to regulate payment service providers and develop a national payment system. Section 49 sets specific conditions for issuing electronic money, supplementing the general licensing requirements. The Marshall Islands Sovereign Currency Act of 2018 declared a blockchain-based digital decentralized currency, "The Sovereign" (SOV), as legal tender.

11. Taxation

The rise of the digital economy offers significant economic benefits but presents unique challenges for domestic and international taxation. Indirect taxes of e-commerce and digital trade, particularly Value Added Tax (VAT), play a crucial role in digital trade by ensuring that Governments can generate revenue from online transactions. This is increasingly vital as e-commerce grows. VAT provides a way of levelling the playing field between domestic and foreign suppliers by requiring businesses to collect tax on sales, thus contributing to public finances. It is particularly important in the context of digital goods and services, where traditional tax systems may struggle to adapt. VAT can also enhance compliance and reduce tax evasion by establishing clear guidelines for taxation in cross-border transactions, promoting fair competition among businesses.

However, tax administrations face several challenges in effectively implementing VAT in the digital economy. One significant hurdle is the difficulty in tracking and taxing cross-border transactions, especially with the rise of digital platforms that operate globally. Many countries lack the necessary infrastructure and expertise to monitor online sales effectively and this can lead to revenue losses. Additionally, varying VAT rates and regulations across jurisdictions create complexity for businesses operating in multiple markets, increasing compliance costs and the risk of errors. Tax administrations also grapple with the fast-paced evolution of technology and the emergence of new business models, which can outstrip existing tax frameworks. Addressing these challenges requires enhanced cooperation between countries, investment in technology, and the development of more adaptable tax policies.[12]

The majority of Pacific Island countries maintain indirect tax legislation and frameworks, yet they do not address the emerging issues related to the taxation of e-commerce and digital trade. However, a number of developments have taken place, including the draft VAT bill in Fiji, which proposes that non-resident digital service providers serving Fijian consumers must register for and collect VAT. Palau introduced a 10 per cent goods and services tax (PGST) on 1 January 2023, with non-residents required to register if their sales surpass $300,000, following a consultation process initiated on 25 July 2022.

> Although some countries are making progress, the lack of e-commerce tax frameworks limits government revenues.

12 See *Indirect Taxation of E-Commerce and Digital Trade: Implications for Developing Countries* at https://unctad.org/system/files/official-document/dtlecde2024d2_en.pdf

Table 3
Status of cyberlaws in the Pacific (November 2024)

Jurisdiction	E-transactions / E-signatures	Online consumer protection	Data protection and privacy	Cybercrime and cybersecurity	IP and copyright	Online content regulation	Domain names	Online dispute resolution	Digital ID	E-payments	Taxation
Cook Islands	Limited / None	Partial	Limited / None	Limited / None	Partial	Limited / None	Comprehensive	Limited / None	Limited / None	Limited / None	Comprehensive
Fiji	Comprehensive	Partial	Limited / None	Comprehensive	Partial	Comprehensive	Limited / None	Limited / None	Limited / None	Partial	Partial
Kiribati	Comprehensive	Partial	Limited / None	Comprehensive	Partial	Limited / None	Partial	Limited / None	Limited / None	Partial	Partial
Marshall Islands	Limited / None	Partial	Limited / None	Limited / None	Partial	Partial	Limited / None	Limited / None	Limited / None	Partial	Limited / None
Federated States of Micronesia	Limited / None	Partial	Limited / None	Limited / None	Partial	Limited / None	Limited / None	Limited / None	Limited / None	Limited / None	Limited / None
Nauru	Limited / None	Comprehensive	Limited / None	Comprehensive	Partial	Partial	Limited / None	Limited / None	Limited / None	Limited / None	Limited / None
Niue	Limited / None	Limited / None	Limited / None	Limited / None	Partial	Limited / None	Partial	Limited / None	Limited / None	Limited / None	Partial
Palau	Limited / None	Partial	Partial	Comprehensive	Partial	Limited / None	Limited / None	Limited / None	Comprehensive	Partial	Partial
Papua New Guinea	Comprehensive	Partial	Limited / None	Comprehensive	Comprehensive	Partial	Partial	Limited / None	Comprehensive	Partial	Comprehensive
Samoa	Comprehensive	Partial	Limited / None	Comprehensive	Partial	Partial	Limited / None	Limited / None	Limited / None	Limited / None	Comprehensive
Solomon Islands	Limited / None	Limited / None	Limited / None	Partial	Partial	Limited / None	Limited / None	Limited / None	Limited / None	Partial	Partial
Timor-Leste	Comprehensive	Partial	Partial	Partial	Partial	Limited / None	Limited / None	Limited / None	Limited / None	Limited / None	Limited / None
Tonga	Limited / None	Partial	Limited / None	Comprehensive	Partial	Comprehensive	Comprehensive	Limited / None	Limited / None	Limited / None	Partial
Tuvalu	Partial	Limited / None	Limited / None	Partial	Partial	Partial	Partial	Limited / None	Limited / None	Limited / None	Partial
Vanuatu	Comprehensive	Limited / None	Limited / None	Comprehensive	Partial	Partial	Limited / None	Limited / None	Limited / None	Limited / None	Partial

Source: UNCTAD.
Note: "Comprehensive" refers to countries with comprehensive laws specifically dedicated to addressing the legal area(s) in question. "Partial" indicates that the legal framework addresses certain aspects of the digital environment but is not fully comprehensive. "Limited/None" indicates that there are no laws specifically dedicated to addressing digital or online environments in relation to the legal area(s) in question. However, certain relevant provisions may be found in other general legislation.

For further information, please refer to the country reports for detailed insights.

E. Way Forward: Strategic Level Reforms for a Thriving Digital Economy

The rise of the digital economy in the Pacific presents significant policy challenges that require comprehensive regulatory solutions. For now, the status of laws and regulations varies significantly across the region, with countries progressing at different paces and exhibiting varying level of implementation capacity (see Part II). Accelerating legal reforms is crucial to fully harness the potential of e-commerce and digital trade.

To support these efforts, Governments from Pacific countries should consider a balanced approach between short-term goals focusing on capacity-building, stakeholder engagement and foundational legal updates; and long-term goals, which address structural reforms, regional harmonization and which require sustained effort, collaboration and resources over time.

This balanced approach will ensure policymakers can deliver rapid results while setting the foundation for transformative, long-term progress.

Short terms goals should aim to:

Strengthen implementation capacity:

- Invest in capacity-building initiatives to enhance the ability of Governments and institutions to effectively prepare and implement and enforce policies, laws and regulations for online activities.

Engage stakeholders in policy development:

- Involve key stakeholders, the private sector, civil society, trade authorities, including customs, and international partners in developing and refining e-commerce regulations.
- Collaborate closely with stakeholders, including trade and customs authorities, during the development and implementation of digital regulations, particularly focusing on initiatives like Single Window systems.
- Establish a national interagency task force with a clear and comprehensive mandate, addressing both domestic and cross-border issues, and supported at the highest levels of government.
- Foster public awareness and engagement through policy dialogues and forums –both at international and regional levels– to facilitate the sharing of best practices and promote mutual recognition of laws. This will also enhance cross-border connectivity for customs agencies and interoperability of e-platforms.

Ensure that laws and regulations clearly define who and what is being regulated, creating alignment across regulations:

- Strengthen collaboration across regulatory agencies using tools such as codes of conduct, regulatory sandboxes and multi-agency and fora for cross-sector cooperation at national, regional and global levels.
- Address ambiguities in existing regulations to ensure clarity and alignment.

Leverage international standards and best practices and leverage assistance from development partners:

- Align domestic e-commerce laws with international standards and best practices (table 3), while adapting them to the local context.
- Draw upon experiences from other regions and seek support from development partners for technical expertise and funding.

Develop comprehensive domestic legal frameworks:

- Focus on developing and implementing laws to address key areas identified as gaps in this study. The legal frameworks must balance strong regulatory foundations –to ensure the security and validity of e-transactions– with flexible, practical processes that promote e-transactions and digital trade across multiple sectors and industries.
- Benchmark existing laws and regulations against digital trade provisions of bilateral and regional agreements, whenever relevant, to ensure competitiveness and alignment with global trends.
- While the different legal subject areas covered in this study are examined independently, any law reform efforts must recognise that these areas often intersect or overlap. For example, advances in digital ID and e-payment may pose challenges to the protections intended by data privacy regulations. Lawmakers must always remain mindful of how reform in one legal field affects the values protected in another.
- Build freely accessible and up-to-date on-line legal databases (e.g., through PacLII) [13] to enhance transparency and global sharing. Many, though not all jurisdictions, currently provide such resources.

Long-term goals:

Harmonize legal frameworks across the region:

- Work towards coordinated regional law reforms to create a predictable and standardized regulatory environment for digital trade and consumer protection. Harmonizing legal frameworks brings several benefits, such as increased efficiency, predictability, collaboration, enforcement abilities and resource pooling.
- Collaborate with regional organizations (e.g., Pacific Islands Forum Secretariat, PIFS) and partners to integrate legal framework development into regional strategies and roadmaps. The Pacific Regional E-commerce Strategy does incorporate legal framework development as a key priority area and aims to standardize e-commerce laws across Pacific nations to increase predictability, facilitate digital trade and strengthen consumer protection. By harmonizing these frameworks, the strategy seeks to create a consistent regulatory environment that supports both local and cross-border e-commerce growth. In this context, fostering regional collaboration between Governments, businesses, PIFS and development partners to create a more predictable legal environment for businesses and consumers, facilitate digital trade and enhance regional integration will be key. Efforts such as the 2023 regional workshop with support from organizations including the Commonwealth Secretariat and UNCTAD have been pivotal. They have helped stakeholders establish a foundation for coherent legal reforms across the region and promote better coordination in the development of e-commerce law.

[13] See http://www.paclii.org/.

Participate in regional and international initiatives:

- Engage in global and regional initiatives to foster policy coherence and interoperability in data, systems and platforms.
- Promote knowledge exchange and consensus on regulatory approaches to enhance cross-border trade and consumer protection.

Incorporate the "resilience principle" into technological and legal frameworks:

- Introduce laws that embed cybersecurity and resilience principles, ensuring systems can withstand disruptions. The "resilience principle" imposes cybersecurity obligations on users meaning that all reasonable steps must be taken to ensure system integrity, and to avoid manipulation and unlawful access.
- Promote the adoption of back-up features and system integrity obligations to minimize societal vulnerabilities, e.g., where a particular system is attacked or otherwise fails. Sovereignty and resilience considerations can form part of the assessment of any adoption of both hardware and software systems.

In terms of technical assistance, development partners such as the Asian Development Bank (ADB), Commonwealth Secretariat, the Council of Europe (CoE), the United Nations Capital Development Fund (UNCDF), UNCITRAL, UNCTAD, and the World Bank provide a range of technical assistance to Pacific Island countries to develop the necessary legal and regulatory frameworks to support digital trade and economic growth. Additionally, bilateral support from Australia and the European Union further strengthens this work.

Mapping these efforts will help align these initiatives and ensure coordinated and cohesive progress.

1. Commonwealth Secretariat

- Commonwealth Connectivity Agenda (CCA) for Trade and Investment[14] (2018) aims to boost trade and investment links across the Commonwealth and is structured around five clusters:
  - Physical connectivity, focusing on digital infrastructure and led by The Gambia.
  - Digital connectivity, focusing on digital transformation and the digital economy and led by Mauritius.
  - Regulatory connectivity focusing on the regulatory environment for MSMEs and led by Barbados.
  - Business-to-business connectivity focusing on improving Commonwealth business links and led by Bangladesh.
  - Supply-side connectivity focusing on participation and upgrading of MSMEs in agribusiness value chains and led by Vanuatu.
- These activities are further supported by the Commonwealth Working Group on Legal Reform and Digitalization. This working group has recently been established to provide resources, advocacy, technical assistance, information sharing and policy recommendations to assist Commonwealth member countries in navigating the legal reforms necessary for a smooth transition from paper-based to paperless trade. The working group is presently working on the development of a Commonwealth Model Law on Digital Trade that is in alignment with UNCITRAL Model Law on Electronic Transferable Records (MLETR) and the best international practice standards, and which will support legal reform initiatives.

14 See: https://thecommonwealth.org/connectivity-agenda#:~:text=The%20Commonwealth%20Connectivity%20Agenda%20for,undertake%20domestic%20reforms%20through%20digitalisation.

Table 4
Regional and international instruments relevant to digital trade in Pacific Small Island Developing States

Key legal areas	Regional and international instruments
e-transactions	• UNCITRAL Model Law on Electronic Commerce (1996)[15] • UNCITRAL Model Law on Electronic Signatures (2001)[16] • UNCITRAL Convention on the Use of Electronic Communications in International Contracts (2005)[17] • UNCITRAL Model Law on Electronic Transferable Records (2017)[18] • UNCITRAL Model Law on Automated Contracting (2024) • Trade Agreements with e-commerce chapters: Regional Comprehensive Economic Partnership, The Comprehensive and Progressive Agreement for Trans–Pacific Partnership • UN Framework Agreement on Facilitation of Cross-border Paperless Trade in Asia and the Pacific 2016[19] • Commonwealth Model Law on Electronic Transactions, 2017[20]
Cybercrime	• Council of Europe Budapest Convention on Cybercrime[21] • Commonwealth Model Law on Computer and Computer-related Crime • United Nations Convention against Cybercrime: Strengthening International Cooperation for Combating Certain Crimes Committed by Means of Information and Communications Technology Systems and for the Sharing of Evidence in Electronic Form of Serious Crimes, adopted in August 2024[22]
Data protection	• Council of Europe Convention for the Protection of Individuals with regard to Automatic Processing of Personal Data (Convention 108+)[23] • APEC Privacy Framework[24] • Commonwealth Secretariat's Model Provisions on Data Protection 2023[25] • OECD Guidelines on the Protection of Privacy and Transborder Flows of Personal Data[26]
Online consumer protection	• United Nations Guidelines for Consumer Protection (UNGCP) [27]
Intellectual property	• WTO Agreement on Trade-Related Aspects of Intellectual Property Rights (TRIPS) • The WIPO Convention (1996)
Online dispute resolution	• OECD Online Dispute Resolution Framework (OECD ODR Framework) • UNCITRAL Technical Notes on Online Dispute Resolution (2016) • UNCITRAL Working Group III (Online Dispute Resolution) procedural rules for ODR to settle disputes arising from ecommerce. See A/CN.9/WG.III/WP.133 and Add.1 • APEC Collaborative Framework for Online Dispute Resolution of Cross-Border Business-to-Business Disputes
Digital identity	• UNCITRAL Model Law on the Use and Cross-border Recognition of Identity Management and Trust Services (2022) • OECD Recommendation on the Governance of Digital Identity 2023.

15 See: https://uncitral.un.org/sites/uncitral.un.org/files/media-documents/uncitral/en/19-04970_ebook.pdf
16 See: https://uncitral.un.org/sites/uncitral.un.org/files/media-documents/uncitral/en/ml-elecsig-e.pdf
17 See: https://uncitral.un.org/sites/uncitral.un.org/files/media-documents/uncitral/en/06-57452_ebook.pdf
18 See: https://uncitral.un.org/sites/uncitral.un.org/files/media-documents/uncitral/en/mletr_ebook_e.pdf
19 See: https://treaties.un.org/Pages/ViewDetails.aspx?src=TREATY&mtdsg_no=X-20&chapter=10&clang=_en
20 See at https://production-new-commonwealth-files.s3.eu-west-2.amazonaws.com/migrated/key_reform_pdfs/P15370_8_ROL_Model_Bill_Electronic_Transactions_0.pdf
21 See: https://www.coe.int/en/web/cybercrime/the-budapest-convention
22 See: https://documents.un.org/doc/undoc/gen/v24/055/48/pdf/v2405548.pdf
23 See: Council of Europe Convention for the Protection of Individuals with regard to Automatic Processing of Personal Data (Convention 108+)
24 See: https://www.apec.org/publications/2005/12/apec-privacy-framework
25 See: Commonwealth Secretariat's Model Provisions on Data Protection 2023
26 See: https://www.oecd-ilibrary.org/science-and-technology/oecd-guidelines-on-the-protection-of-privacy-and-transborder-flows-of-personal-data_9789264196391-en
27 The Guidelines encourage Member States to develop strong consumer protection policies, tailored to their specific economic, social, and environmental contexts. Particularly, under Section III, General Principles, it is emphasized that Member States should aim to ensure a level of protection for consumers engaging in electronic commerce that is equivalent to that provided in traditional commerce. Moreover, Guidelines 63 to 65 of the UNGCP call on Member States to strengthen consumer protection in electronic commerce by ensuring that the level of protection for online consumers is equivalent to that in traditional commerce (Guideline 63). This involves reviewing and adapting existing policies to address the unique challenges of e-commerce and making sure consumers and businesses are aware of their rights and obligations in the digital marketplace (Guideline 64).The Guidelines are based on the OECD Guidelines for Consumer Protection in the Context of Electronic Commerce. See: https://unctad.org/topic/competition-and-consumer-protection/un-guidelines-for-consumer-protection.

- **Capacity-building:** The CCA offers capacity-building workshops to policy and law makers involved in ICTs and digital trade. Activities include regional trainings for representatives of Pacific Island Member States in conjunction with other development partners such as UNCTAD, and providing technical assistance to Fiji, Samoa, Tonga, and Vanuatu to develop legal frameworks. This support includes conducting national e-commerce legislative gap analyses, policy development in key areas such as digital finance and consumer protections within digital markets, as well as technical assistance to develop laws and regulations.

2. Council of Europe

- **Legislation:** The Cybercrime Programme Office of the Council of Europe (C-PROC),[28] through its two projects, the Global Action on Cybercrime Enhanced (GLACY-e) and "Octopus",[29] provides technical assistance to interested Pacific Island countries in aligning their national legislation on cybercrime and electronic evidence with international standards, particularly the Convention on Cybercrime (Budapest Convention).
- **Capacity-building:** In the Pacific, C-PROC focuses on enhancing the knowledge of law enforcement agencies (LEAs) and judicial authorities by increasing their understanding of the provisions of the Budapest Convention, promoting international cooperation and supporting the implementation of international standards at national level in its partner countries. Currently, C-PROC works with four Pacific countries: Fiji, Kiribati, Tonga, and Vanuatu, and engages with the PILON Working Group on Cybercrime. Through its capacity-building projects, C-PROC has facilitated dialogue between national stakeholders in Fiji, Kiribati, Nauru, Papua New Guinea, Tonga, and Vanuatu, focusing on the development and implementation of legislation on cybercrime and electronic evidence.

3. UNCDF

- **Technical assistance:** As part of the Pacific Digital Economy Programme (PDEP), UNCDF will provide technical support to the Ministry of Communication and Aviation of Solomon Islands to develop a national policy on data protection. The draft will encompass personal and enterprise protection, as well as covering national and cross border transfers, adhering to OECD (Organisation of Economic Co-operation and Development) guidelines and the Budapest Convention.
- **Legislation:** As part of the Pacific Digital Economy Programme, UNCDF is supporting the Consumer Council of Fiji to conduct a comprehensive mapping and review of existing fraud, scam, and consumer protection legislation on online platforms in the country. The work will also identify gaps and weaknesses, benchmark against international best practices and propose necessary legal reforms to ensure a robust and effective legal framework for the country.

4. UNCITRAL

- **Model laws:** UNCITRAL provides model laws and legal standards that Pacific Island countries can adopt to develop their e-commerce legislation. The UNCITRAL Model Laws on Electronic Commerce and on Electronic Signatures and the United Nations Convention on the Use of Electronic Communications in International Contracts are key resources that help countries establish legal frameworks for electronic transactions.

---

28 Cybercrime Programme Office (C-PROC), Council of Europe, https://www.coe.int/en/web/cybercrime/cybercrime-office-c-proc-

29 Global Action on Cybercrime Enhanced (GLACY-e), https://www.coe.int/en/web/cybercrime/glacy-e. Octopus Project

- **Capacity-building**: UNCITRAL offers training and workshops to government officials and legal practitioners in the Pacific, helping them understand and implement international e-commerce laws and best practices. The UNCITRAL Secretariat has assisted Fiji, Kiribati and Papua New Guinea in the preparation of the Electronic Transaction Bill and the consideration of the adoption of the United Nations Convention on the Use of Electronic Communications in International Contracts. Similar work is ongoing for Tonga and Tuvalu.

5. UNCTAD

- **Technical assistance**: UNCTAD provides tailored support for the development and reform of domestic and regional e-commerce laws. UNCTAD, as part of the activities under PDEP and in collaboration with UNCDF (which will create a national policy on data protection), will draft data protection legislation in Solomon Islands. UNCTAD also offered analysis and recommendations on the legal frameworks to support the development of e-commerce and digital trade through eTrade Readiness Assessments and e-commerce strategies.
- **Capacity-building:** In the context of PDEP and in collaboration with eTrade for All partners and other development partners, including UNCDF, the Commonwealth Secretariat, UNCITRAL and the Pacific Island Forum, UNCTAD conducted numerous workshops for Pacific Island policymakers and legal practitioners in 2023. These workshops offered hands-on training on key legal issues surrounding e-commerce and digital trade. Additionally, UNCTAD offered an online training course on digital identity as part of capacity-building activities conducted for SIDS.

6. World Bank

- **Technical assistance:** The World Bank offers capacity-building and policy reform dialogues in three main areas:

  i. Support for the development of unique national ID in several Pacific SIDS, looking at legislation and regulations for digital ID (Kiribati, the Marshall Islands, the Federated States of Micronesia, and Tonga). Recent activity in the region includes the conclusion of a new investment project agreement with the Government of Samoa to implement the National Digital ID (NDID) Bill with funds to develop the system, carry out a national registration campaign, and pilot some use cases for NDID.

  ii. Large portfolio of technical assistance and lending operations related to national payment systems, almost all of which address data and digital issues. Technical assistance in this area includes legislative, strategic, and regulatory assistance. In several countries, the Bank conducts payments reforms as prior actions in support operations. The World Bank is also supporting Governments in the region with financing to implement the systems, especially under a new project on Correspondent Banking Relationships which will also be heavily engaged in payment systems.

  iii. Data privacy and protection reforms: some work is ongoing in Fiji with the development of a national data privacy and protection policy.

  iv. Consumer protection, with a focus in some instances on financial consumer protection (which includes digital finance), e.g., in Papua New Guinea and upcoming Fiji.

Part 2

Legal frameworks across Pacific jurisdictions

This part provides an overview of the relevant legislation in each Pacific jurisdiction in the areas of e-transactions, e-signatures, consumer protection, data protection and privacy, cybercrime and cybersecurity, intellectual property and copyright, online content regulation, domain names, online dispute resolution, digital ID, e-payments and taxation.

A. Cook Islands

The legal system of the Cook Islands is rooted in common law.[30] From 1901 to 1965, the Cook Islands were a dependent territory of New Zealand. In 1965, the Cook Islands became self-governing in free association with New Zealand, adopting its own Constitution and establishing its own Government. Today, the legal framework of the Cook Islands includes the Constitution as the supreme law, Acts of the Cook Islands Legislative Assembly and Parliament, and pre-1965 Ordinances. Additionally, the legal framework incorporates applicable Acts of the New Zealand Parliament, English common law and equity, and ancient customs and usage of the Cook Islands people.

The Cook Islands' National Digital Strategy for 2024 to 2030 was released in February 2024 and outlines six strategic priorities. The strategy includes a number of key actions, such as conducting a legal and regulatory gap analysis to identify priorities and ensuring the legal framework remains up to date. There is a focus on developing robust cybersecurity measures and enhancing digital safety awareness. A supportive framework for the local digital private sector will boost economic diversification. Laws will be updated to support innovations such as ridesharing (sharing a vehicle with others, typically facilitated by an app or digital platform). In addition, a comprehensive open data approach has been proposed to foster collaboration between the Government and the private sector.

The digital strategy reinforces the Cook Islands National ICT Policy 2023–2027, and the 2023 E-Commerce Acceleration Work Plan. The work plan outlines a phased strategy to develop a robust e-commerce ecosystem through Government and private sector collaboration and details key actions and implementation priorities. The work plan adopts the recommendations from the Legislative Gap Assessment , which identified key gaps in the Cook Islands' legal and regulatory framework for e-commerce.

1. E-transactions /E-signatures

The laws of the Cook Islands do not comprehensively address e-transactions or e-signatures. Instead, e-transactions are governed by general law as it applies to both online and offline transactions. Certain laws impact or facilitate e-transactions in specific contexts, such as the Financial Transactions Reporting Act 2017 and the Companies Act 2017; for example the Financial Transactions Reporting Act 2017 addresses electronic funds transfers.

2. Consumer protection

The Cook Islands has enacted several pieces of legislation that offer consumer protection in e-commerce. The Fair Trading Act 2008 applies to advertising and selling of goods and services by traders (private sales are not covered). It addresses matters such as traders misleading consumers, providing false information or using unfair trading practices. It also sets consumer information standards and regulates product safety.

Additional protection for consumers both online and offline, is provided in the form of the Consumer Guarantees Act 2008. This law includes guarantees in respect of the supply of goods and services. For example, goods must be of an acceptable quality (Section 6), be fit for a particular purpose (s. 8) and correspond with descriptions (s. 9) and samples (s. 10). Similarly, services must be fit for a particular purpose (s. 29) and provided with reasonable care and skill (s. 28).

[30] Online legal information resources seem incomplete: https://parliament.gov.ck/parliamentary-business/acts/; http://www.paclii.org/countries/ck.html.

Furthermore, Part 3 Subpart 3, of the Telecommunications Act 2019 provides consumer protection in relation to anyone classed as a "service provider". The term "service provider" means "any person that provides or offers to provide a telecommunications service in the Cook Islands" (s. 5(1)). Part 3 Subpart 3, of the Telecommunications Act 2019 regulates, for example, misleading or deceptive conduct by such persons (s. 14), service quality indicators (s. 15), customer service guarantees (s. 16), and mandates that standard terms and conditions must be fair, reasonable and expressed in plain language (s. 19(1)).

While neither limited to consumers, nor specifically enacted in relation to e-commerce, the Sale of Goods Act 1908 (New Zealand) (extended by Section 638 of the Cook Islands Act) provides implied conditions and warranties that may still benefit online consumers. These general protections, though initially devised for traditional commerce, can also extend to certain aspects of digital transactions.

The Cook Islands is a founding member of the Pacific Island Network of Competition Consumer and Economic Regulators (PINCCER).[31]

3. Data protection and privacy

The Cook Islands' laws do not include any specific legislation for data protection and privacy.

However, Part 3 Subpart 4, of the Telecommunications Act 2019 addresses confidentiality, privacy and unsolicited communications (spam) in a rudimentary manner. While the provisions are sector-specific and relatively general, they touch on key considerations often found in data privacy laws. For example, under Part 3 Subpart 4 of the Telecommunications Act 2019, a service provider "must take all reasonable steps to ensure the privacy of its customers' communications" (s. 23(1)), and "must not collect, use, maintain, or disclose information about a customer for any purpose, except with the customer's consent" (s. 24(1)(a). Further, focus is placed on accuracy and completeness (s. 24(2)), access, correction and removal (s. 24(3)) and information to be disclosed to customers (s. 24(4)).

Other Acts, including the Digital Registers Act 2011 (Section 8) and the Competition and Regulatory Act 2019 (Section 34) have a limited impact on the protection of data privacy within their specific areas of operation. Spam is also specifically regulated in the comprehensive Spam Act of 2008, which is modelled on the Australian Spam Act 2003.

4. Cybercrime and cybersecurity

The Cook Islands does not have specific legislation addressing cybercrime or cybersecurity. However, cybercrime provisions are included in Subpart 9: Offences involving computers of the Crimes Amendment Bill 2017.[32] Provisions stipulate offences ranging from accessing computer systems for dishonest purposes;[33] accessing computer systems without authorization;[34] and illegal data access and interference.[35]

Additional rules relevant to the online context are found in the Terrorism Suppression Act 2004, which includes rules relating to "the recruitment of persons to be members of terrorist groups" (Section 16), and the exchange of information relating to terrorist groups and terrorist acts (s. 34).

In the context of cybercrime, the Tainted Cryptocurrency Recovery Bill 2023 is particularly noteworthy. This Bill has

31 See https://www.mted.gov.to/index.php/2023/11/07/press-release/.
32 See https://parliament.gov.ck/wp-content/uploads/2018/12/Crimes-Bill-2017-final.pdf.
33 The Crimes Amendment Bill 2017, Subpart 9, 189.
34 The Crimes Amendment Bill 2017, Subpart 9, 192.
35 The Crimes Amendment Bill 2017, Subpart 9, 193 and 195.

extraterritorial scope and is aimed at"the detection, investigation of, seizure and forfeiture of cryptocurrency that is, or represents the proceeds of proscribed conduct."[36] However, it should be noted that at the time of writing, the Government of the Cook Islands has decided to withdraw the Bill for redrafting.

Cybersecurity is not specifically regulated. However, Part 3 Subpart 4, of the Telecommunications Act 2019 mandates that a service provider "must apply appropriate security safeguards to prevent the collection, use, maintenance, or disclosure of information about a customer without the customer's consent." (Section 24(1)(b). Finally, as noted above, spam is also specifically regulated in the comprehensive Spam Act of 2008.

The Cook Islands is a member of the Pacific Islands Law Officers' Network.[37]

5. Intellectual property and copyright

Intellectual property and copyright are addressed in the Copyright Act 2013 and the Traditional Knowledge Act 2013. These Acts are technology-neutral and do not specifically address e-commerce. The Cook Islands is a Member State of the World Intellectual Property Organization (WIPO) and has acceded to the Berne Convention for the Protection of Literary and Artistic Works.

6. Regulating online content

Freedom of speech and expression is established under the Constitution (Section 64(1)(e)). Other Constitutionally guaranteed rights of relevance include the freedom of thought, conscience, and religion (s. 64(1)(d)), as well as the freedom of peaceful assembly and association (s. 64(1)(f)) and the right of the individual to equality before the law and to the protection of the law (s. 64(1)(b)).

Other, more specific laws also impact online content regulation. Provisions included in the Crimes Amendment Bill 2017 provide partial protection for online users. Regulation of online content may also be influenced by the Traditional Knowledge Act 2013 that includes the regulation of registered traditional knowledge. For example, Section 10(1) makes clear that "No person may treat or deal with registered traditional knowledge in a manner that is prejudicial to the honour or reputation of the rights-holder or rights-holders of the knowledge."

7. Domain names

Internet domain administration is overseen by the Competition and Regulatory Authority (CRA),[38] established under the Competition and Regulatory Authority Act 2019.

Part 7 of the Telecommunications Act 2019 regulates domain administration for the ".ck" top-level domain. Section 58 specifies that the responsibility for the allocation and registration of ".ck" domains may be transferred to a nominated person, subject to necessary approvals and consents being given by the Internet Assigned Numbers Authority (IANA), and terms agreed with IANA. Further, under Section 58(4), the CRA must monitor compliance by any nominated person with the requirements of Section 58.

8. Online dispute resolution

The laws of the Cook Islands do not specifically address online dispute resolution.

9. Digital ID

The laws of the Cook Islands do not specifically address digital ID.

36 See https://parliamentci.wpenginepowered.com/wp-content/uploads/2023/12/Explanatory-Note-Tainted-Cryptocurrency-Recovery-Bill-No.-14-1-1-21.pdf.

37 See https://pilonsec.org/about/members/.

38 See https://cra.org.ck/.

10. E-payments

The laws of the Cook Islands do not specifically address e-payments.

11. Taxation

The Ministry of Finance and Economic Management oversees taxation and customs.[39]

The laws of the Cook Islands do not specifically address taxation of e-commerce. Important legislation includes the Value Added Tax Act 1997 as amended, and the Income Tax Act 1997, as amended.

The Cook Islands is a member of the OECD and Group of Twenty Inclusive Framework on Base Erosion and Profit Shifting (BEPS),[40] and of the Pacific Islands Tax Administrators Association (PITAA).[41]

39 See http://www.mfem.gov.ck/.

40 See https://www.oecd.org/tax/beps/about/.

41 See https://pitaa.org/.

B. Fiji

The legal system in Fiji blends common law –derived from its British colonial past– with customary law rooted in indigenous Fijian traditions.[42] The Constitution of Fiji serves as the supreme legal authority, guiding governance and fundamental rights. Statutory laws enacted by Parliament build on these foundations. Courts, including the Supreme Court, the Court of Appeal and the High Court ensure the application of these laws, while customary practices influence areas such as land ownership and inheritance.

The draft Fiji National Digital Strategy outlines a comprehensive roadmap for the country and proposes a holistic approach involving all sectors of Government and society to ensure inclusive transformation. Advancing cybersecurity regulations and strengthening the e-commerce legal framework are key considerations within this strategy.

Fiji conducted a second Cybersecurity Maturity Model review with the Oceania Cyber Security Centre, which assessed and enhanced cybersecurity for public and private sectors. The review, alongside stakeholder consultations, identified challenges, priorities and best practices and informed the development of the Fiji National E-commerce Strategy 2025–2029. The initiative was supported by UN Trade and Development and endorsed by Cabinet through Decision 170/2024. The National Development Plan 2025–2029 and Vision 2050 for Fiji also merit attention[43] as they offer a holistic view of the laws governing e-payments, digital virtual assets and the economic dimensions of trade-related areas.

Additionally, a forthcoming National Cybersecurity Strategy will further bolster Fijian defences against evolving cyber threats, ensuring security of digital platforms and e-commerce systems. This strategy, along with the Cybercrime Act 2021, will provide a comprehensive legal and policy framework that underpins the country's efforts to promote trust and security in the digital economy.

1. E-transactions /E-signatures

Fiji has adopted legislation based on or influenced by the UNCITRAL Model Law on Electronic Commerce (1996)[44] in the form of the Electronic Transactions Act 2008. This Act was substantially amended in 2017 via the Electronic Transactions (Amendment) Act 2017. The Act now also gives effect to the domestic implementation of the 2005 United Nations Convention on the Use of Electronic Communications in International Contracts of UNCITRAL, to which Fiji is a party. The amended Electronic Transactions Act provides comprehensive regulation for matters such as the validity of electronic transactions (s. 5), time and place of dispatch and receipt (ss. 6–9), attribution (s. 11), invitations to make offers (s. 12A), in writing requirements (s. 13), and electronic evidence (s. 18). E-signatures are regulated under Section 14 of the Electronic Transactions Act, which adopts a technology-neutral approach. This allows the use of e-signatures without prescribing detailed requirements for a valid signature.

2. Consumer protection

The Consumer Council of Fiji (CCF) is a statutory body established under the Consumer Council of Fiji Act 1976 (Cap. 235).[45] Under the requirements of the Act, the Council is guided by the General

42 A legal information database is available at https://www.laws.gov.fj/.
43 See https://www.finance.gov.fj/national-development-plan-2/#1726102354566-0f435183-3aaa.
44 See https://uncitral.un.org/en/texts/ecommerce/modellaw/electronic_commerce/status.
45 See http://www.consumersfiji.org/.

Principles and Guidelines for Consumer Protection of the United Nations.[46] The Consumer Council of Fiji is a member of Consumers International.[47]

In addition, the Fijian Competition and Consumer Commission (FCCC) –an independent statutory body established under Section 7 of the Fijian Competition and Consumer Commission Act 2010– promotes competition and an informed market, encourages fair trade in markets and protects customers and businesses from restrictive practices.[48]

Consumer protection is provided via a patchwork of laws such as the Consumer Credit Act 1999. As far as goods are concerned, consumers may rely on the conditions and warranties of the Sale of Goods Act 1985. However, the most important instrument is the already noted Fijian Competition and Consumer Commission Act 2010. This Act provides comparatively extensive consumer protection addressing matters such as misleading or deceptive conduct (s. 75), unconscionable conduct (s. 76), referral selling (s. 87), unsolicited goods and services (ss. 92–94), as well as conditions and warranties in consumer transactions (ss. 111–118).

There is also important sectoral protection. Specifically, under Section 54 of the Telecommunications Act 2008, consumers enjoy certain protections in relation to service providers that supply telecommunications services, such as the need to provide terms and conditions in a "simple to understand" manner.

Since 2022, Fiji has been a partner within the International Consumer Protection and Enforcement Network (ICPEN),[49] and is a founding member of the Pacific Island Network of Competition Consumer and Economic Regulators (PINCCER).[50]

3. Data protection and privacy

The Constitution of the Republic of Fiji (2013) provides for a right to privacy, including a right to confidentiality of personal information (Section 24).

Fiji does not have specific data protection or privacy laws. However, certain aspects commonly addressed under data privacy laws are regulated by the Information Act 2018. Section 6 provides a right of access to information held by a public agency, which would enable an individual to access their personal data in a manner similar to that under data privacy laws. In addition, Part 3 regulates requests for the correction or deletion of personal information held by public agencies, which is also a standard right for individuals under data privacy laws.

In addition, the Telecommunications Promulgations 2008 contains obligations for telecommunication service providers regarding customer data confidentiality and consent requirements. Part IV of the Posts and Telecommunications Act 1989 outlines various offences for modification, interception and disclosure of messages. However, these provisions only apply to telecommunications employees.

A selection of other Acts impact data privacy in limited and specific settings: the Banking Act 1995 (Section 27 and Section 71); the Fiji Revenue and Customs Service Act 1998 (Section 52(2)); the Medical and Dental Practitioner Act 2010 (Section 126); the Legal Practitioners Act 2009 (Rules of Professional Conduct and Practice (para 1.4)).[51]

46 See https://unctad.org/system/files/official-document/ditccplpmisc2016d1_en.pdf.

47 A membership organization bringing together over 200 member organisations in more than 100 countries to empower and champion the rights of consumers everywhere. (https://www.consumersinternational.org/who-we-are/).

48 See https://fccc.gov.fj/.

49 See https://icpen.org/who-we-are.

50 See https://www.mted.gov.to/index.php/2023/11/07/press-release/.

51 See https://www.dlapiperdataprotection.com/index.html?c=FJ&c2=&go-button=GO&t=law.

4. Cybercrime and cybersecurity

The Cybercrime Act 2021 has extraterritorial reach (Section 3) and provides a comprehensive and coherent framework on cybercrime and electronic evidence. Its scope covers offences against the confidentiality, integrity and availability of computer data and computer systems (ss. 5–8), including computer-related and content-related offences (ss. 9–10). It also addresses procedural measures (ss. 15–23), international cooperation, preservation and disclosure of data, mutual legal assistance and transborder access to stored computer data with consent or where publicly available (ss. 24–34). Specific offences such as identity theft (s. 11) and theft of telecommunication services (s. 12) are also covered.

Furthermore, in its definition of a "false representation", the False Information Act 2016 – an Act making it an offence to provide false information to the Government– explicitly refers to electronic means such as "e-mail correspondence" and "communication in person, by phone or any electronic means" (Section 2). The Online Safety Act 2018 focuses on certain specific offences. Section 24(1) makes it an offence to post an electronic communication: (a) with the intention to cause harm to an individual; (b) where posting the electronic communication would cause harm to an ordinary reasonable individual in the position of the individual; and (c) where posting the electronic communication causes harm to the individual.[52] Further, Section 25 regulates the posting of an intimate visual recording.

Cybersecurity is partially addressed under the Cybercrime Act 2021 and Part IV of the Posts and Telecommunications Act 1989. A National Cybersecurity Strategy is also under development. This strategy will aim to strengthen the capacity of Fiji to combat evolving cyber threats and includes a cybersecurity maturity assessment to better understand national preparedness. Additionally, Fiji is working on a broader National Digital Strategy (2025–2029) that integrates cybersecurity as a core pillar to safeguard its digital infrastructure and promote trust in its emerging digital economy.

A Memorandum of Understanding between Australia and Fiji was signed in 2024, outlining areas of cooperation. These include support for the computer emergency response team (CERT) in Fiji, strengthening its capabilities and providing assistance in combating cyber incidents. Fiji also contributes resources and expertise regionally through the Pacific Computer Emergency Response Team (PacCERT. However, within PacCERT, operational challenges –mainly due to funding limitations– have affected its activities in recent years. Fiji does not have other specific cybersecurity legislation in place.

The Mutual Assistance in Criminal Matters Act 1997 (amended in 2005) facilitates the provision of assistance to foreign law enforcement and judicial authorities and plays a key role in enabling international cooperation in combating transnational crime, including cybercrime. Furthermore, Fiji recently deposited its instrument of accession to the Budapest Convention on Cybercrime, marking a significant step to enhancing international cooperation in addressing cybercrime.

Fiji is also a member of the Pacific Islands Law Officers' Network, and actively engages in regional and international cybersecurity efforts. [53]

5. Intellectual property and copyright

Major law reform was gazetted (officially published) in 2021. Intellectual property and copyright is primarily addressed in the Copyright Act 1999 (Act No. 11 of 1999),

[52] At first glance, Section 24(1)(c) appears to make it an offence to harm oneself by posting an electronic communication. However, it is doubtful that that is the correct interpretation.

[53] See https://pilonsec.org/about/members/.

the Designs Act 2021 (Act No. 38 of 2021), the Patents Act 2021 (Act No. 37 of 2021) and the Trademarks Act 2021 (Act No. 36 of 2021) (the latter not in force at time of writing). These Acts are technology-neutral.

Fiji is a Member State of WIPO and has acceded to the Berne Convention for the Protection of Literary and Artistic Works.

6. Online content regulation

Freedom of speech, expression and publication is established under the Constitution (Section 17). Other Constitutionally guaranteed rights of particular relevance online include the freedom of religion, conscience, and belief (s. 22), as well as the freedom of assembly (s. 18) and association (s. 19) and the right of the equality and freedom from discrimination (s. 26).

Several Acts –applicable both offline and online– impact online content, such as the Defamation Act 1971, the Gaming Act 2009, and the Television and Online Streaming Act 1992.

In the context of online content regulation, the Online Safety Act 2018 plays a central role. This Act establishes the Online Safety Commission[54] and provides important procedural and substantive rules. The Act has extraterritorial applicability with some limitations (Section 4), and the stated objectives of the Act include: promoting responsible online behaviour and online safety (s. 3(a)); promoting a safe online culture and environment that addresses cyberbullying, cyber stalking, Internet trolling and exposure to offensive or harmful content particularly in respect of children (s. 3(b)); deterring harm caused to individuals by electronic communications (s. 3(c)); and providing an efficient means of redress for such individuals (s. 3(d)).

7. Domain names

The country code top-level domain (ccTLD) for Fiji is ".fj". Domain names cannot be registered directly under .fj; they must be registered as third-level domains, such as ".com.fj" or ".org.fj". The domain ".fj" was registered in 1992 and is currently administered by the University of the South Pacific IT Services.[55] The ITC Services Department[56] of the Fiji Government is the sole authority of registration and administration for all ".gov.fj" domains.

8. Online dispute resolution

The laws of Fiji do not specifically address online dispute resolution.

9. Digital ID

The laws of Fiji do not specifically address digital ID.

10. E-Payments

The National Payment System Act 2021[57] aims "to empower the Reserve Bank of Fiji to develop and implement a national payment system framework to regulate payment service providers operating wholly or partially in Fiji."[58] Section 49 specifically governs the issuance of electronic money, outlining conditions to ensure secure and reliable issuance. These requirements, in addition to the general licensing obligations for payment service providers, are designed to enhance consumer trust, safeguard digital transactions, and foster the growth of e-payments and financial inclusion across Fiji.

54 See https://onlinesafetycommission.com/.
55 See https://www.usp.ac.fj/information-technology-services/fj-domain-name-registry/. See specifically: https://www.domains.fj/index.php.
56 See http://www.itc.gov.fj/.
57 See https://www.rbf.gov.fj/national-payment-system-act-2021-act-no-4-of-2021/.
58 See https://www.dataguidance.com/news/fiji-parliament-passes-national-payment-system-act-2021.

11. Taxation

Fiji does not currently have any tax law specific to e-commerce. However, the Fiji Revenue and Customs Service (FRCS) is working on a draft VAT bill, which, if approved, will require non-resident providers of digital services to register and collect VAT. FRCS has emphasized the taxability of online business income since 2018, urging compliance with VAT obligations.[59] Recently, FRCS clarified that VAT was extended to personal imports via online purchases, addressing unfair market practices. Taxation is regulated via several Acts such as the Income Tax Act 2015, and the Value Added Tax Act 1991 (as amended). All businesses operating in Fiji must register with FRCS for tax purposes. Fiji is a member of the Pacific Islands Tax Administrators Association (PITAA).[60]

59 See https://www.frcs.org.fj/wp-content/uploads/2018/12/Tax-TalkOnline-Business.pdf.
60 See https://pitaa.org/.

C. Kiribati

Sources of law in Kiribati include the Constitution, Acts of Parliament, English common law and equity, pre-Independence British Acts, and customary law.[61] Upon independence on 12 July 1979, Kiribati adopted a written Constitution as the supreme law and retained existing laws until repealed. The Laws of Kiribati Act 1989 further defined the legal framework, emphasizing the application of customary law alongside the Constitution, Acts of the Maneaba ni Maungatabu (House of Assembly), subsidiary legislation, and retained British laws until repealed.

In 2019, the Government of Kiribati published its National ICT Policy[62] which was based on an original version from 2011. The policy addresses several aspects of e-commerce and related fields. Included in the policy are goals that will establish comprehensive cyberlaws, data protection and privacy laws, electronic transaction laws and a revised Evidence Act.[63] The same goals are listed in the Communications Commission Strategic Plan for the fiscal years 2020 to 2024.[64]

The Digital Government Act 2023 –part of the Kiribati Digital Government Master Plan 2021– aims to transform public service delivery and enhance good governance through digital solutions.

1. E-transactions /E-signatures

Kiribati adopted the Electronic Transactions Act in 2021.[65] This Act provides legal recognition and status to the use of electronic communications and signatures (Part 2 and Part 4 respectively) and regulates matters such as electronic contracting (Part 3), electronic transferable records (Part 5), and electronic exchanges with public bodies (Part 6).

Kiribati is a party to the United Nations Convention on the Use of Electronic Communications in International Contracts (New York, 2005) and this instrument has now entered into force. Kiribati has also adopted the UNCITRAL Model Law on Electronic Transferable Records (2017).

2. Consumer protection

The Consumer Protection Act 2001, as amended, is the main consumer protection instrument in Kiribati. However, the Act focuses on traditional commerce and lacks the specificity needed to fully cover online and digital transactions.

The Ministry of Commerce, Industry and Cooperatives (MCIC)[66] was established under this Act and has a specific consumer protection unit.[67] MCIC is responsible for consumer protection and administration in upholding the rights of consumers, fair trading and statutory warranties. As amended, the Consumer Protection Act 2001 includes a broad definition of who is classed as a consumer. Section 2 states: "…"consumer" means a person or enterprise who acquires goods or services from any supplier, including a manufacturer, trader, or provider of services or advice". The Act requires that traders display certain information (Sections 17 and 19) and that

61 Online legal information resources seem incomplete, see https://kiribati.gov.ki/my-government/acts; https://www.parliament.gov.ki/acts-kiribati.
62 See https://www.mict.gov.ki/download/file/fid/295.
63 See https://www.mict.gov.ki/download/file/fid/295 at page 27
64 See http://www.cck.ki/images/jdownloads/Final_CCK_Strategic_Plan_2020_to_2024.doc.
65 See https://www.president.gov.ki/images/Gazettes/gaz2021/Electronic_Transactions_Act_2021.pdf.
66 See https://mcic.gov.ki/.
67 See https://mcic.gov.ki/consumer-protection-unit/.

they issue receipts (s. 18). Furthermore, under the Act, "No person shall, in the course of a trade or business, engage in conduct that is misleading or deceptive or is likely to mislead or deceive any purchaser or possible purchaser and any person who contravenes this Section commits an offence against this Act." (s. 20). Finally, the Act implies certain warranties (s. 21), addresses a range of specific forms of misleading conduct (s. 22, and ss. 24–25), and imposes requirements relating to the availability of spares or replacements for goods of a reasonable quantity (s. 23).

At the time of writing, work is ongoing to replace the 2001 Act with a more modern instrument (Consumer Protection Bill 2023) that specifically addresses online consumer issues.

The Communications Act 2012 provides that the Communications Commission of Kiribati may make consumer protection rules regulating unsolicited communication, confidentiality of subscriber information, terms of service, the handling of disputes and complaints, directory assistance and quality of service (ss. 53, 54, 58, 59 and 60).

Finally, Kiribati is a founding member of the Pacific Island Network of Competition Consumer and Economic Regulators (PINCCER).[68]

3. Data protection vand privacy

Although efforts are underway to develop a comprehensive data privacy law, Kiribati currently lacks specific data protection and privacy legislation. As noted in the National ICT Policy in 2019, "More measures are needed to protect citizens' rights when their [...] personal data is stored in private or government databases."[69] However, some provisions provide a degree of privacy protection. For example, via the 2018 amendment of the Penal Code, it is an offence to "operate a device" for the purpose of observing or filming another person (Section 135D).

A further example can be found in Section 110A of the Communications Act 2012 (as amended in 2017), which regulates unauthorized interception of communications, as well as Sections 54–55 that impose requirements of confidentiality of customer information (s. 54) and communications (s. 55) in the specific context of communications services. Section 54 is particularly noteworthy as it addresses several typical data privacy matters such as consent, collection, use and disclosure.

4. Cybercrime and cybersecurity

Kiribati introduced a modern Cybercrime Act in 2021[70] –with limited extraterritorial reach (Section 4)– addressing matters such as unauthorized access, interception, data interference, systems interference (ss. 7–10), computer-related forgery and fraud (ss. 12–13), procedural law matters (ss. 22–29) and international cooperation (ss. 30–36). The Kiribati Cybercrime Act draws upon both the Budapest Convention on Cybercrime and the Commonwealth Model Law on Computer and Computer-Related Crime. In this context, reference may also be made to the Mutual Assistance in Criminal Matters Act, 2003 (No. 6 of 2003), and the Measures to Combat Terrorism and Transnational Organised Crime Act 2005.

A range of crimes relevant to the online environment are addressed in the Communications Act 2012 (as amended in 2017); most importantly, Part XIV, Computer Misuse, including Sections 107–111 addressing offences against computer data and systems, and Sections 112–114 regarding content-related offences.

68 See https://www.mted.gov.to/index.php/2023/11/07/press-release/.
69 See https://www.micttd.gov.ki/sites/default/files/National%20ICT%20Policy.pdf, page 13.
70 The United Kingdom Online Safety Act, An Act To Provide For The Prevention, Investigation And Suppression Of Computer Related Offences And For Other Connected Purposes (No.10 of 2021).

Turning to cybersecurity, the National Cybersecurity Strategy 2020 is a key document.[71] This strategy builds on existing policies, setting goals and objectives for maximizing ICT safety and security. It aligns with the National ICT Policy 2019 and the United Nations Sustainable Development Goals.

Further, the Digital Government Act 2023 establishes the Kiribati National Computer Emergency Response Team (Sections 20–21) and regulates the unlawful use of top secret and confidential computer data (s. 46). The already noted provisions of the Communications Act 2012 (as amended in 2017) have obvious cybersecurity relevance; see especially Section 54(1)(b) which imposes a requirement to implement "appropriate security safeguards".

Building on this foundation, the creation of a Cybersecurity Act is a critical next step in strengthening the legal framework in Kiribati. This Act, currently being developed under the Kiribati Digital Government Project, financed by the World Bank, will complement the existing Cybercrime Act and the National Cybersecurity Strategy. The process involves collaboration between technical assistance providers and the Digital Transformation Office (DTO) under the Ministry of Information, Communications, and Transport. The Cybersecurity Act is expected to outline specific cybersecurity measures, roles and responsibilities and provide a more comprehensive and structured approach to managing cybersecurity risks. It will further enhance the nation's resilience against cyber threats.

Kiribati is a member of the Pacific Islands Law Officers' Network,[72] and has been invited to accede to the Budapest Convention.

5. Intellectual property and copyright

Intellectual property law in Kiribati is under review at the time of writing. Intellectual property and copyright are primarily addressed in the Copyright Act 2018, the Trademark Act 2019, the Registration of United Kingdom Patent Ordinance (Cap. 87) and the Registration of United Kingdom Designs Protection (Cap. 99). These instruments are generally technology-neutral and, in most instances, do not specifically address matters related to e-commerce. However, examples can be found –such as the regulation of the circumvention of technological protection measures in Section 25 of the Copyright Act 2018– that show direct engagement with technology-driven issues.

Kiribati is a Member State of WIPO and has acceded to several key international treaties and conventions, including the Berne Convention for the Protection of Literary and Artistic Works, the Marrakesh Treaty, the WIPO Copyright Treaty (WCT), the WIPO Performances and Phonograms Treaty (WPPT), the Beijing Treaty on Audiovisual Performances (BTAP), and the Paris Convention for the Protection of Industrial Property, in relation to other intellectual property laws.

These international instruments establish obligations that Kiribati must consider, particularly when adapting its intellectual property framework to address evolving technology and e-commerce challenges. The Intellectual Property Division within the Ministry of Commerce, Industry and Cooperatives is responsible for providing services in accordance with these agreements.

71 See https://www.mict.gov.ki/download/file/fid/300.

72 See https://pilonsec.org/about/members/.

6. Online content regulation

Whilst there is no specific piece of legislation addressing illegal and restricted content, Chapter II of the Constitution of Kiribati specifically caters for certain freedoms that are of particular relevance in the context of online content regulation. Freedom of expression (Section 12), assembly and association (s. 13), freedom of conscience, including freedom of thought and of religion (s. 11), secure protection of laws (s. 10), and protection against discrimination (s. 15) are all covered.

In addition, the Communications Act 2012 (as amended in 2017) regulates certain content-related offences; specifically, copyright infringements (s. 112), distribution and exhibition of obscene matter (s. 113), and child pornography (s. 114).

7. Domain names

The country code top-level domain for Kiribati is ".ki". Domains can be registered directly under ".ki" or as third-level domains, such as "com.ki", "biz.ki", or "org.ki". The ".ki" top-level domain was introduced in 1995 and is currently administered by the Communications Commission of Kiribati.[73] The Digital Government Act 2023 includes some rules relating to the Government domain .gov.ki (Section 38).

8. Online dispute resolution

The laws of Kiribati do not specifically address online dispute resolution.

9. Digital ID

While Kiribati has adopted a National Identity Registration Act 2018, the laws of Kiribati do not specifically address digital ID.

10. E-payments

The laws of Kiribati do not specifically address e-payments. However, Section 33(2)(b) of the Kiribati Digital Government Act 2023 specifies the establishment of a National Government Portal, which is currently being developed by the Digital Transformation Office. This Section addresses e-payment services as part of the functionalities of the National Digital Government Portal. Specifically, it mentions:

1. Electronic receipt of payment services: This indicates the ability to receive confirmations or receipts for payments made electronically.
2. Electronic payment services options: This refers to providing various methods for making electronic payments through the portal.
3. Electronic monitoring and tracking of service payment status: This feature allows users to track the status of their payments.

11. Taxation

The laws of Kiribati do not specifically address taxation of e-commerce. Important legislation includes the Value Added Tax Act 2013 as amended, and the Income Tax Act 1989 as amended. The former is under review at the time of writing. Kiribati is a member of the Pacific Islands Tax Administrators Association (PITAA).[74]

73 See https://www.cck.ki/; see also: https://www.cck.ki/index.php/downloads/finish/24-all-services/61-kiribati-domain-name-service-agreement-for-2nd-level-domain-names.

74 See https://pitaa.org/.

D. Marshall Islands

The Republic of the Marshall Islands is a self-governing country under the Compact of Free Association with the United States, wherein the United States manages defence and national security. The country's legal system, governed by its own Constitution, is primarily influenced by United States common law, customary law, traditional practices and statutes.[75]

The Marshall Islands has a digital strategy in place as part of its broader development initiatives. The Government recently launched Agenda 2030: A Pathway for a Resilient and Prosperous Future, which outlines various reforms and projects aimed at modernization, including a significant focus on digital transformation. This framework aligns with the National Strategic Plan 2020–2030 and integrates ongoing efforts related to global initiatives such as the Sustainable Development Goals. The plan includes 35 priority areas that address pressing developmental challenges and emphasizes the need for a comprehensive approach to digitalization across various sectors. Moreover, the Marshall Islands is working towards establishing a national digital payments system to improve financial inclusion and transparency. This initiative leverages blockchain technology and aims to enhance economic activity, especially for marginalized communities.

Previously, a national ICT policy was adopted in 2012 to liberalize the market by enhancing private participation and investment in ICT services, strengthening existing service providers and fostering competition.

1. E-transactions /E-signatures

The Marshall Islands has not adopted any specific legislation for e-transactions or e-signatures. However, recent relevant legislation, seen in the Decentralized Autonomous Organization Act 2022 allows for decentralized autonomous organizations (DAOs), which are blockchain-based companies where members collectively make decisions. DAOs rely heavily on blockchain technology, smart contracts and digital signatures to operate and use e-transactions and e-signatures to facilitate secure decision-making. DAOs can be established and managed as domestic limited liability companies under the Marshall Islands' Limited Liability Company Act 1996.

The technology-neutral Consumer Protection Act is the main instrument protecting consumers in the Marshall Islands. Section 403 declares as unlawful a range of unfair methods of competition and unfair or deceptive acts or practices in the conduct of any trade of commerce. This including passing off; deceptive representations or designations of geographic origin; breach of an express or implied warranty; representing that goods or services are of a particular standard, quality, or grade; representing that goods are of a particular style or model if they are of another; engaging in any act or practice which is unfair or deceptive to the consumer; and engaging in any other conduct which similarly creates a likelihood of confusion of or misunderstanding. The same Act also established the Consumer Protection Board.

It should also be noted that the Uniform Commercial Code (Reference) Act 2018 provides that "Subject to customary law and traditional practice, the Constitution, or Acts, of the Nitijela, with respect to the commercial matters, the courts of the Republic may look to, but shall not be bound by, Uniform Commercial Code" (Section 102). In particular, Article 2, Sales of the Uniform Commercial Code, can also be relevant in this context.

75 A legal information database is available at https://rmiparliament.org/cms/legislation.html?view=acts_alpha.

2. Consumer protection

The technology-neutral *Consumer Protection Act* is the main instruments protecting consumers in the RMI. In Section 403, it declares as unlawful a range of unfair methods of competition and unfair or deceptive acts or practices in the conduct of any trade of commerce; including e.g., passing off, deceptive representations or designations of geographic origin, breach of an express or implied warranty, representing that goods or services are of a particular standard, quality, or grade, or that goods are of a particular style or model, if they are of another, engaging in any act or practice which is unfair or deceptive to the consumer, and engaging in any other conduct which similarly creates a likelihood of confusion of or misunderstanding. The same Act also established the Consumer Protection Board.

It should also be noted that, the *Uniform Commercial Code (Reference) Act 2018* provides that "Subject to customary law and traditional practice, the Constitution, or Acts, of the Nitijela, with respect to the commercial matters, the courts of the Republic may look to, but shall not be bound by, Uniform Commercial Code" (Section 102). In particular, Article 2, Sales of the Uniform Commercial Code may provide some assistance in this context.

3. Data protection and privacy

The Constitution of the Republic of the Marshall Islands expressly protects privacy in declaring that "all persons shall be free from unreasonable intrusions into their privacy" (Section 13).

The Marshall Islands does not have specific data protection laws. However, some regulations partially overlap with data protection. These include the Exchange of Information (Confidentiality) Act 1989 and the technology-neutral Criminal Code 2011 which addresses violations of privacy (Section 250.12).

Under the Child Rights Protection Act 2015, children (anyone under 18 years) are specifically protected in their right to privacy and against unlawful attacks on their reputation (Section 1010). Additionally, s.1114 of the Rights of Persons with Disabilities Act 2015 emphasizes that "Persons with disabilities have the right, equally with others, to privacy".

4. Cybercrime and cybersecurity

While authorities in the Marshall Islands have been working on a Cybercrime Bill since 2019, the country still has no laws covering the main powers related to cybercrime and electronic evidence.[76]

The technology-neutral Criminal Code 2011 has extraterritorial reach (Section 1.03) and contains rules governing several types of criminal offences that may be committed online. Examples include theft by deception (s.223.3), tampering with records (s. 224.5), deceptive business practices (s.224.8), stalking (s.250.5), and harassment (s.250.4). The harassment provision specifically references harassment via "electronic mail".

The Marshall Islands does not have a national Computer Incident Response Team (CIRT)[77]. The Marshall Islands is a member of the Pacific Islands Law Officers' Network.[78]

5. Intellectual property and copyright

Intellectual property and copyright are addressed in the Unauthorized Copies of Recorded Materials Act 1991. This instrument is technology-neutral and does not specifically address e-commerce related matters. The Republic of the Marshall Islands is a Member State of WIPO.

---

76 See https://www.coe.int/en/web/octopus/-/marshall-islands?redirect=https://www.coe.int/en/web/octopus/country-wiki?p_p_id=101_INSTANCE_AZnxfNT8Y3Zl&p_p_lifecycle=0&p_p_state=normal&p_p_mode=view&p_p_col_id=column-4&p_p_col_pos=1&p_p_col_count=2.

77 See https://www.itu.int/en/ITU-D/Cybersecurity/Documents/Country_Profiles/Marshall_Islands.pdf.

78 See https://pilonsec.org/about/members/.

6. Online content regulation

The Constitution of the Republic of the Marshall Islands protects freedoms relevant to online content regulation. Freedom of thought, speech, press, religion, assembly, association, and petition are all covered in Section 1. Further, Section 12 ensures equal protection under the law and freedom from discrimination. Section 14 ensures access to judicial processes. These rights are safeguarded under the Human Rights Committee Act 2015.

The Marshall Islands does not have specific laws regulating online content. However, several technology-neutral laws may impact it. For example, Section 215 of the Elections Offenses Act makes it a misdemeanour to provide false and misleading information, while the Gaming and Recreation Prohibition Act 1998 bans the promotion of gaming or gambling activities.

7. Domain names

The country code top-level domain for the RMI is ".mh". The Internet Assigned Numbers Authority indicates "http://www.nic.net.mh/" as the URL for registration services. However this link is inactive at the time of writing.[79] The public bodies of the Marshall Islands seem to prefer gTLDs (generic top-level domains such as .org or .com). For example the Parliament uses ".org",[80] and the Ministry of Finance uses ".com".[81]

8. Online dispute resolution

The Marshall Islands has not adopted any specific legislation for online dispute resolution.

9. Digital ID

The Marshall Islands has not adopted any legislation specifically for digital ID.

10. E-payments

In 2018, the Marshall Islands made headlines with its bold move to adopt blockchain technology as a national currency. With a population of 53,000, the nation does not issue its own currency and relies on the United States dollar. The Declaration and Issuance of the Sovereign Currency Act 2018 aimed to establish a digital decentralized currency, based on blockchain technology, as the legal tender of the Marshall Islands (s.302). The currency, called "The Sovereign" or ("SOV")[82] was issued via the SOV Foundation,[83] the non-profit organization that governs the network. SOV aims to promote economic independence, reduce reliance on the United States Dollar and improve financial inclusion.

However, the International Monetary Fund (IMF) has repeatedly warned against issuance of the SOV. It has highlighted that the SOV would pose significant risks to macroeconomic and financial stability, as well as financial integrity. The IMF is also concerned that the Marshall Islands does not have the legal, regulatory or institutional framework to accommodate SOV issuance and manage associated risks.[84]

11. Taxation

The laws of the Marshall Islands do not specifically address taxation of e-commerce. Important legislation includes the Tax Collection Act, and the Income Tax Act 1989. The Marshall Islands is a member of the Pacific Islands Tax Administrators Association (PITAA).[85]

79 Last checked 8th January 2025.
80 See Government website of the Marshall Islands, https://rmiparliament.org/cms/
81 See https://www.rmimof.com.[
82 See https://web.archive.org/web/20180301224603/http://pr.blonde20.com/media-kit-rmi/.
83 See https://sov.foundation/.
84 See https://www.imf.org/en/News/Articles/2021/03/22/pr2173-marshall-islands-imf-staff-completes-2021-article-iv-mission; https://www.imf.org/en/News/Articles/2023/09/21/pr23319-marshall-islands-imf-executive-board-concludes-article-iv-consultation-marshall-islands.
85 See https://pitaa.org/.

E. Federated States of Micronesia

The legal system in the Federated States of Micronesia is a mixed system of common and customary law.[86] Sources of law include national and state constitutions, legislation, treaties, traditions, common law, Micronesian court decisions and certain Trust Territory of the Pacific Islands (TTPI) statutes.

The laws of the Federated States of Micronesia safeguard traditions and customs. While the Constitution doesn't define "law", it requires courts to interpret it in harmony with customs and the social and geographical context of Micronesia. English prevails in legal interpretations, despite local language translations. State Constitutions are in English and in local languages. The Federated States of Micronesia has a unified legal framework across national and state levels, although it is recognized as comprising multiple Governmental entities. Customary practices hold significant legal weight at both national and state levels.

The National ICT and Telecommunications Policy for the Federated States of Micronesia was first published in 2012 and amended in July 2021. One of its goals is to create "an enabling ICT environment through policy reform and improvements in legal frameworks".[87] The policy covers several specific goals such as ICT awareness workshops for legislatures; encouraging the private sector to develop e-money such as mobile money and debit cards to easily make online payments; online help support for doctors; guiding principles for patient information confidentiality relating to the use of electronic patient or medical records; new laws in relation to non-discrimination, cybercrime, child protection, spam, evidence, copyright and piracy (e.g., for software, films, etc.); and a right to information.

1. E-transactions /E-signatures

The laws of the Federated States of Micronesia do not specifically address e-transactions or e-signatures.

2. Consumer protection

The Consumer Protection Act 1970, as amended, is the primary consumer protection instrument in the Federated States of Micronesia. In this Act, Section 103 regulates a wide range of unfair methods of competition and unfair or deceptive acts or practices, that when carried out in the conduct of any trade or commerce are declared to be unlawful. Most importantly, Section 103 addresses passing off (s. 103(1)), the causing of a likelihood of confusion or of misunderstanding as to specific defined matters such as certification of goods or services (s. 103(2–3)), a range of false or deceptive representations as to specific matters such as that goods or services are of a particular standard, quality, or grade (s. 103(4-8)), certain types of advertising (s. 103(9-10)), and regulations for price reductions (s. 103(11)).

In addition to these relatively specialized rules targeting specific types of conduct, are much broader rules found in Section 103(12) and in Section 103(13). The former makes it unlawful to engage "in any other conduct which similarly creates a likelihood of confusion or of misunderstanding", while the latter makes it unlawful to engage "in any act or practice which is unfair or deceptive to the consumer".

Finally, the International Trade Act ("Deceptive Labelling of Imports Act") makes it "unlawful for any person to import into the

[86] A legal information database is available at http://fsmlaw.org/index.htm.
[87] See https://fsm-data.sprep.org/dataset/fsm-national-ict-and-telecommunications-policy-2012.

Federated States of Micronesia for sale any foreign product with a name, mark, symbol, language, or identification of any sort which falsely suggests manufacture, growth, or assembly of the product in the Federated States of Micronesia" (Section 403).

3. Data protection and privacy

The Federated States of Micronesia lack specific data protection or privacy regulation. However, Sections 349 and 350 of Title 21 of the Code of the Federated States of Micronesia oblige telecommunications providers to ensure confidentiality of customer information and communications. Section 349 of Title 21 prohibits collecting, using, storing or sharing information about a customer for any purpose without the customer's consent. It also requires proper security measures to prevent unauthorized access or use.

In addition, the Federated States of Micronesia torts law (which deals with civil wrongs like harm to individuals or their rights) recognises a tort of invasion of privacy.[88] There has been no evidence that the tort of invasion of privacy has been applied in an online context. However, when this tort is used in cases involving the Internet, it may be impacted by the Uniform Single Publication Act, which also addresses privacy violations.[89]

The Declaration of Rights found in the Constitution of the Federated States of Micronesia (Article IV) specifically provides for the protection of privacy (Section 5). However, this provision is more limited than similar rights in other jurisdictions, as it only mentions privacy in terms of protecting "their persons, houses, papers, and other possessions". While case law suggests that "[a] citizen is entitled to protection of the privacy which he seeks to maintain even in a public place",[90] it is not clear the extent to which the right of privacy in Section 5 provides protection online.

The Telecommunications Act prohibits the unauthorized publication of communications (Section 105).

4. Cybercrime and cybersecurity

Although authorities in the Federated States of Micronesia have been working on cybercrime legislation since 2019,[91] the country still lacks laws covering substantive or procedural powers for cybercrime and electronic evidence. Further, there is no specific legislation addressing cybersecurity.

The Crimes Act –with its extraterritorial reach (Section 103)– contains some provisions of specific relevance to cybercrime, such as the provisions of Chapter 9 relating to money laundering and proceeds of crime. The Federated States of Micronesia is a member of the Pacific Islands Law Officers' Network.[92]

The Federated States of Micronesia does not have a framework for addressing cybersecurity, although steps to change this are underway. The country has developed cybersecurity initiatives and guidelines as part of its broader digital development and security efforts but it does not yet have a comprehensive national cybersecurity law.

88 *Mauricio v. Phoenix of Micronesia*, Inc., 8 FSM R. 411 (Pon. 1998); *Nethon v. Mobil Oil Micronesia*, Inc., 6 FSM R. 451 (Chk. 1994); *Helgenberger v. Helgenberger*, 22 FSM R. 244 (Pon. 2019). See also: http://fsmlaw.org/fsm/decisions/digest/pdf/TORTS.pdf.

89 Code of The Federated States Of Micronesia, Title 6. Judicial Procedure, Chapter 11. Uniform Single Publication Act (ss. 1101–1102).

90 *FSM v. Tipen*, 1 FSM Intrm. 79, 86 (Pon. 1982).

91 See https://www.coe.int/en/web/octopus/-/micronesia-federal-states-of-?redirect=https://www.coe.int/en/web/octopus/country-wiki?p_p_id=101_INSTANCE_AZnxfNT8Y3Zl&p_p_lifecycle=0&p_p_state=normal&p_p_mode=view&p_p_col_id=column-4&p_p_col_pos=1&p_p_col_count=2.

92 See https://pilonsec.org/about/members/.

5. Intellectual property and copyright

Title 35 of the Code of the Federated States of Micronesia is labelled "Copyrights, Patents and Trademarks". It is drafted in technology-neutral language, and is the main instrument in the Federated States of Micronesia for regulating intellectual property and copyright. However, despite its title, it only contains rules regarding copyright; the Federated States of Micronesia has no trademark or patent law.

6. Online content regulation

The Declaration of Rights found in the Constitution of the Federated States of Micronesia (Article IV) specifically provides for freedom of expression, peaceable assembly, association or petition (Section 1). Other Constitutionally guaranteed rights of particular relevance online include the freedom of religion (s. 2), the rights to due process of law and the equal protection of the laws (s. 3), and protection against discrimination (s. 4).

While technology-neutral, the Crimes Act –with its extraterritorial reach (Section 103)– contains some provisions relevant to the context of online content regulation. For example, Article 403 relates to content advocating armed insurrection.

7. Domain names

The Federated States of Micronesia Telecommunications Corporation administers the country code top-level domain ".fm".

8. Online dispute resolution

The laws of the Federated States of Micronesia do not specifically address online dispute resolution.

9. Digital ID

The laws of the Federated States of Micronesia do not specifically address digital ID.

10. E-payments

The laws of the Federated States of Micronesia do not specifically address e-payments.

11. Taxation

Taxation is regulated under the technology-neutral Taxation and Customs Act. The Federated States of Micronesia is a member of the Pacific Islands Tax Administrators Association (PITAA).[93]

93 See https://pitaa.org/.

F. Nauru

The legal system of Nauru is based on English common law and acts passed by the Nauru Parliament. Full recognition of Nauru customary law is acknowledged in the Custom and Adopted Laws Act of 1971.[94]

Nauru has implemented the Nauru Digital Strategy 2020–2025. This initiative is designed to enhance the country's digital landscape by promoting innovation, improving infrastructure and fostering a supportive environment for startups and technological advancements.

The Communications and Broadcasting Act 2018 is a significant piece of legislation affecting several areas discussed in more detail below. The Act also establishes the Nauru Communications Authority.

1. E-transactions /E-signatures

The laws of Nauru do not specifically address e-transactions and e-signatures. However, as noted below, the Crimes Act 2016 addresses identity crime (Sections 193–197) and makes specific reference to digital signatures.

2. Consumer protection

Research identified a modern level of consumer protection law in Nauru, seen in the Consumer Protection Act 2024. The Act does not have any specific provisions for online transactions, cross-border protections or digital transparency. However, it does contain provisions for restrictive business conduct and practices (Part 3); misleading conduct (Part 4); pricing and standards of goods and services (Parts 5 and 6); consumer complaints (Part 7); enforcement (Part 8); and establishing a Consumer Protection Authority (Part 2).[95]

Similar consumer protection measures can be found in other legislation. Section 89 of the Communications and Broadcasting Act 2018 prohibits discriminatory behaviour by service providers with substantial market power in a communication services market, ensuring equal terms of service supply.

Additional consumer protections can be found in the regulation of "false trade description" in the Commerce (Trade Descriptions) Act 1905 (Act No. 16 of 1905), and the provisions of the Mercantile Act 1912 No 38. Both can be helpful to consumers, either directly or indirectly.

3. Data protection and privacy

Nauru lacks comprehensive data protection and privacy laws and the Constitution of Nauru does not expressly refer to a right to privacy. Instead it references "respect for his private and family life" in the Preamble to Part II. As a result, these aspects are only partially protected through a patchwork of legal provisions.

The Crimes Act 2016 makes it an offence, in certain circumstances, to observe private acts by others (Section 110), to take images of private acts without consent (s. 111), to take images of private parts without consent (s. 112), and to install a device to facilitate observation or image-taking (s. 113).[96]

The Communications and Broadcasting Act 2018 regulates confidentiality of subscribers' information (Section 48) and confidentiality of subscriber communications (s. 49).

In Nauru, the Drones Act 2018 prohibits photography, filming and recording (Section 13) and surveillance of residential premises (s. 16) in certain circumstances.

The Official Information Act 1976 No 16 imposes restrictions on the use and disclosure of "official information". Defined in Section 2, this refers to "any document or information which a person has obtained,

94 A legal information database is available at http://ronlaw.gov.nr/nauru_lpms/.

95 See http://ronlaw.gov.nr/nauru_lpms/files/em/a3b2bc0f6e2ce297a97b21351f3ce250.pdf.

96 Sections 121–124 contain specific rules for this kind of behaviour in relation to children.

or to which he or she has had access, by reason of his or her being, or having been, a public officer or a government contractor". These restrictions may offer some data privacy protection in certain circumstances.

Finally, Section 52 of the Public Enterprises Act 2019 No 11 contains an obligation that –apart from in a few specified exceptions– directors and employees of a public enterprise "shall not for any purpose use or knowingly disclose any information, document or communication of which he or she becomes aware through his or her connection with the public enterprise".

4. Cybercrime and cybersecurity

The Nauru Cybercrime Act 2015 – with extraterritorial reach (Section 4) addresses a wide range of offences, such as illegal access, interception, data interference, and system interference (ss. 6-8 and 10), as well as spam (s. 18), data espionage (s. 9), computer-related forgery and fraud (ss. 12-13). Further, this Act deals with child pornography (s. 14), the publication of indecent or obscene information or material in electronic form (s. 16) and makes clear that "the fact that evidence has been generated from an electronic system does not prevent that evidence from being admissible" (s. 5). The Cybercrime Act 2015 also regulates the liability of access providers (s. 32), hosting providers (s. 33), caching providers (s. 34), hyperlinks providers (s. 35), search engine providers (s. 36), and outlines monitoring obligations (s. 37).

The Communications and Broadcasting Act 2018 includes offences relating to communications and other information (Section 70) and on interfering or modification of communication (s. 71). Part 15 of that Act governs what may be required of service providers in the case of national security concerns (s. 106), national emergencies or states of disaster (s. 107).

In addition, Section 15 of the Counter Terrorism and Transnational Organised Crime Act 2004 makes it an offence to recruit persons to be members of terrorist groups or to participate in terrorist acts.

In criminal law, it is also important to mention the Mutual Assistance in Criminal Matters Act 2004 No 16 (and the associated Mutual Assistance in Criminal Matters Regulations 2023), and the Counter Terrorism and Transnational Organised Crime Act 2004.

In June 2023, the modern Anti-Money Laundering and Targeted Financial Sanctions Act 2023 –applying to "virtual assets" amongst other areas– came into effect. The technology-neutral Crimes Act 2016 –with its extraterritorial scope (Sections 5-7)– addresses various crimes that may be committed online. For example, Section 61 makes it an offence to encourage suicide; Section 86 regulates stalking; Section 181 deals with blackmail; Sections 249 to 254 address defamation; and Sections 193 to 197 regulate identity crime and makes specific reference to digital signatures.

Part 8 of the Crimes Act 2016 regulates offences relating to certain types of offensive material such as pornography (Section 139) and abuse material (s. 140). Importantly, Part 8 also addresses the distribution of images of private acts (s. 146) and the threat of doing so (s. 147). Amendments in 2020 – in the form of the Crimes (Amendment) Act 2020– include provisions expressly dealing with online activities. Section 243A deals with seditious offences, making clear that a person commits an offence if the person with seditious intention "utters or livestreams any seditious words or information including through the media or any other digital or electronic device or means" (s. 243A(1)(b).[97] For these matters, the Crimes (Amendment) Act 2020 also introduces extended jurisdiction.[98] Nauru is a member of the Pacific Islands Law Officers' Network.[99]

97 Section 243A(1)(c and d) also refer to the online context.

98 Section 243D states: "A person commits an offence against the provisions of this Part: (a) whether or not the conduct constituting the alleged offence occurs in the Republic; and (b) whether or not a result of the conduct constituting the alleged offence occurs in the Republic."

99 See https://pilonsec.org/about/members/.

5. Intellectual property and copyright

In Nauru, intellectual property and copyright are addressed in the Patents Registration Act 1973, the Copyright Act 2019 and the Trademarks Act 2019. The Copyright Act 2019 specifically addresses e-commerce matters. The definition of "artistic, literary or scientific work" includes computer programmes, and "audio-visual work" includes cinematographic elements of computer games (Section 7). Furthermore, Section 36 specifically regulates the copying and adaptation of computer programmes. Nauru is a Member State of WIPO and has acceded to the Berne Convention for the Protection of Literary and Artistic Works.

6. Online content regulation

Freedom of speech and expression is established under the Constitution (Section 12). Other Constitutionally guaranteed rights of particular relevance online include the freedom of conscience, thought and religion (s. 11), as well as the freedom of assembly and association (s. 13) and the right to the secure protection of the law (10).

Part 15 of the Communications and Broadcasting Act 2018 regulates social content regulation. Section 93 empowers the Cabinet to set standards for "content applications services" –including social media platforms, streaming services, or messaging apps– through regulations. These standards apply to all service providers offering such services.

Section 97 relates to the censorship of specific types of content, in particular a "service provider shall not knowingly and with unlawful intent supply any content which: (a) is indecent or obscene; (b) displays excessive violence; (c) is blasphemous; (d) is treasonous or seditious; or (e) will contravene the laws of the Republic." Part 15 of the Communications and Broadcasting Act 2018 does not only restrict certain types of content, it gives the Cabinet power to require a service provider to supply, without any charge, certain content. Under Section 98, the Cabinet may do so in relation to "divine worship content or other content of a religious nature", while Section 99 relates to "content relating to national interest matters". Section 100 states that the "Cabinet may require a service provider to supply with reasonable fee or without charge such educational content as the Cabinet may determine".

Further, the provisions of the Cybercrime Act 2015 that regulate the liability of access providers, hosting providers, caching providers, hyperlinks providers and search engine providers, as well as specifying their monitoring obligations, are relevant in this context.

Finally, Part 16 of the Communications and Broadcasting Act 2018 caters for take-down notices (s. 102), filtering (ss. 103–104) and the mandatory reporting of child pornography material (s. 105).

7. Domain names

The country code top-level domain for Nauru is ".nr". Cenpac Net Inc. is the registry,[100] and the .nr Dispute Resolution Policy is available on their website.[101]

8. Online dispute resolution

The laws of Nauru do not specifically address online dispute resolution.

9. Digital ID

The laws of Nauru do not specifically address digital ID.

10. E-payments

The laws of Nauru do not specifically address e-payments.

100 See https://www.cenpac.net.nr/dns/index.html.
101 See https://www.cenpac.net.nr/dns/dispute.html.

11. Taxation

Cross border e-commerce is not currently subject to tax. Domestic e-commerce would be taxed at ordinary rates of 20 percent for resident taxpayers, 25 percent for non-residents operating through a permanent establishment. Important legislation includes the Business Tax Act 2016, the Employment and Services Tax Act 2014 and the Telecommunications Service Tax Act 2009. The latter imposes a 10 percent tax on the gross revenue of telecommunications service providers defined as "a provider of a telecommunications service or authorized under the Communications and Broadcasting Act 2018" (s. 2), which encompasses certain aspects of digital services. Nauru is a member of the Pacific Islands Tax Administrators Association (PITAA).[102]

[102] See https://pitaa.org/.

G. Niue

The Niue Assembly enacts laws for Niue, with legal sources prioritized in the following order: the Constitution; Acts of the Assembly; Regulations; Niuean custom; and the common law of Niue. Prior to 1974, Acts of the New Zealand Parliament extended to Niue, and some of these laws remain in force, now holding the status of Acts of the Niue Assembly. The Constitution stipulates that a New Zealand Act may apply to Niue as a result of New Zealand legislation after 1974 only if expressly requested and consented to by a resolution of the Niue Assembly, and if the New Zealand Act declares that the request and consent procedure was followed. The Niue Assembly has not made any such requests to date.

The 2016–2026 Niue National Strategic Plan recognizes the importance of ICT to the country's development. The plan states that "ICT development is important for Niue in the changing technological environment and connection to the world". The strategy focuses on providing quality, affordable postal, ICT and broadcasting services.

The Government of Niue completed its National Digital Strategy in 2024 and has recently launched its ICT Policy.

1. E-transactions /E-signatures

There is currently no law covering e-transactions or e-signatures.

2. Consumer protection

Niue lacks specific consumer protection laws. However, consumers do enjoy some protection under the overview of the Sale of Goods Act 1908. Under that Act, certain conditions and warranties are implied, including an implied condition that the goods shall correspond with a given description (Section 15), and implied conditions regarding quality and fitness for purpose (s. 16).

3. Data protection and privacy

There are currently no data protection or privacy laws in Niue.

4. Cybercrime and cybersecurity

Niue has a Cybercrime Bill 2016 which has not been enacted.

Part 5 of the Niue Act 1966 contains some offences that may be applicable in the electronic context. For example, Section 228A regulates wrongful communication, retention or copying of official information. Furthermore, certain provisions of the country's advanced Terrorism Suppression and Transnational Crimes Act 2006 may apply in the context of cyber-related issues. For example, under Section 4(2)(g), the definition of a "terrorist act" includes an act that involves "serious disruption to any system or the provision of services directly related to essential infrastructure". The Mutual Assistance in Criminal Matters Act 1998 may also be noted. Niue is a member of the Pacific Islands Law Officers' Network.[103]

The Niue Cybercrime Policy 2015 is an integral component of the national cybersecurity strategy.

5. Intellectual property and copyright

Section 737 of the Niue Act 1966 makes clear that: "A copyright, design, patent, or

[103] See https://pilonsec.org/about/members/.

trademark protected by New Zealand law shall be accorded the same protection by the courts of Niue as that available in New Zealand under the laws of New Zealand for the time being in force." To this may be added the specific protection provided for certain marks under the Merchandise Marks Act 1954. Niue is a Member State of WIPO and has acceded to the Berne Convention for the Protection of Literary and Artistic Works.

6. Online content regulation

Part 5 of the Niue Act 1966 imposes several restrictions that may amount to online content regulation. Examples include seditious offences (ss. 129–130), inciting or encouraging suicide (s. 149), indecent documents (s. 174), and criminal libel or slander (s. 187).

7. Domain names

The country code top-level domain for Niue is ".nu". Section 30B(1)(b) of the Communications Act 1989 states that "the ccTLD.nu is a National resource for which the prime authority is the Government of Niue".

8. Online dispute resolution

The laws of Niue do not specifically address online dispute resolution.

9. Digital ID

The laws of Niue do not specifically address digital ID.

10. E-payments

The laws of Niue do not specifically address e-payments.

11. Taxation

The laws of Niue do not specifically address taxation of e-commerce. Important legislation includes the Niue Consumption Tax Act 2009 and the Income Tax Act 1961 as amended. Niue is a member of the Pacific Islands Tax Administrators Association (PITAA).[104]

[104] https://pitaa.org/.

H. Palau

The Palau legal system is a mixed legal system of civil, common, and customary law. Laws consist of the Constitution, national laws codified as the Palau National Code, national statutes, ordinances of the 16 states of Palau, rules of common law and equity drawn from the United States, and traditional law. Statutes prevail only to the extent that they are not in conflict with underlying traditional law principles.[105]

Palau is actively developing a digital strategy that encompasses several key initiatives. The country has recently begun transitioning to a 5G network, which is expected to significantly enhance mobile services, disaster response capabilities and overall connectivity. This transition aims to improve various sectors, including tourism, agriculture, education and telemedicine and ultimately transform the digital landscape of Palau. The Government of Palau is currently working on developing a legislative framework and a cybersecurity strategy that align with international standards.

1. E-transactions /E-signatures

There is currently no regulation covering e-transactions or e-signatures.

2. Consumer protection

In the Palau National Code (the "Consumer Protection Act") Chapter 2, Title 11 "Business and Business Regulation", specifically regulates consumer protection. Importantly, Section 203 outlines unlawful acts or practices activities such as: passing off goods or services as those of another (s. 203(a)); causing likelihood of confusion or of misunderstanding as to the source, sponsorship, approval, or certification of goods or services (s. 203(b)); or as to affiliation, connection, or association with, or certification by, another (s. 203(c)). Furthermore, s. 203 addresses deceptive representations or designations of geographic origin (s. 203(d)); representing that goods are original or new if they are not (s. 203(f)); and advertising goods or services with intent not to sell them as advertised (s. 203(i)). In addition to these relatively specific provisions, s. 203 contains two subsections with broad scope. Section 203(m) makes it unlawful to engage "in any other conduct which similarly creates a likelihood of confusion or of misunderstanding"; and s. 203(n) makes it unlawful to engage "in any act or practice which is unfair or deceptive to the consumer."

It must also be noted that Chapter 29 of the Penal Code of the Republic of Palau specifically addresses deceptive business practices (s. 2901) and false advertising (s. 2902).

3. Data protection and privacy

The Constitution of the Republic of Palau does not explicitly protect privacy in the context of data privacy. However, Section 4 states that "Every person has the right to be secure in his person, house, papers and effects against entry, search and seizure".

Palau has a Privacy Act (Title 6, Chapter 2 of the Palau National Code Annotated) that governs Government agencies. As outlined in the Digital Residency Program Cyber Security, the Privacy Act (6 PNCA s. 205–206), requires agencies that maintain personal information to protect this information from loss, unauthorized access, modification, disclosure or other misuse. Agencies cannot retain personal information longer than necessary for its lawful use. Information obtained for one purpose must not be used for another unless one of the

[105] Online legal information resources seem incomplete at https://www.palaugov.pw/document-category/rppls/; see also https://www.palaugov.pw/document-category/bills/; and http://www.paclii.org/pw/legis/num_act/; https://palaulegal.org/ was inaccessible.

following applies: it is publicly available; the individual consents; it is necessary for law enforcement or to prevent a serious threat to public health or safety; the use is directly related to the original purpose; it is for statistical or research purposes without identifying the individual; or it is mandated by a court order.[106]

It must also be noted that Section 4413 of the Penal Code of the Republic of Palau specifically addresses violation of privacy. While predominantly concerned with offline behaviour, some of its provisions could apply online as well. Further, Chapter 10 Financial Institutions, Subchapter VIII of Title 26 –Financial Institutions of the PNC– on Electronic Banking contains a rule that "Banks that permit computer access must provide customers using computer access with a privacy policy statement that includes information to customers regarding what information concerning them is to be collected and how the information will be used, and permit such customers to opt out of information sharing concerning their credit eligibility information by banks with affiliates or with non-affiliated third parties." (Section10.101(c)).

4. Cybercrime and cybersecurity

Palau legislation includes specific cybercrime provisions. Chapter 31 of the Penal Code of the Republic of Palau addresses offences such as computer fraud (ss. 3102–3103), computer damage (ss. 3104–3105), unauthorized computer access (ss. 3109–3111), and using a computer to commit another crime (s. 3106). Notably, Section 3108 establishes extraterritorial jurisdiction, and states "For purposes of prosecution under this part, a person who causes, by any means, the access of a computer, computer system, or computer network in one jurisdiction from another jurisdiction is deemed to have personally accessed the computer, computer system, or computer network in each jurisdiction."

It must also be noted that Chapter 18 of the Penal Code of the Republic of Palau specifically addresses child exploitation, including electronic enticement of a child (ss. 1806–1807) and indecent electronic display to a child (s. 1808). Chapter 33 addresses money laundering and Chapter 22 addresses terrorism, both of which have specific e-aspects: Section 3316 addresses "Misuse of information technology". In addition, it should be noted that the Rules of Criminal Procedure for the Courts of the Republic of Palau[107] specify that: "A judge may consider information communicated by telephone or other reliable electronic means when reviewing a complaint or deciding whether to issue a warrant or summons." (Rule 4.1(a)).

In the area of cybersecurity, Palau does not have a comprehensive cybersecurity law. However, there are generally worded cybersecurity provisions in sector-specific laws, in addition to the relevant provisions of the Penal Code mentioned above. Once again, Chapter 10, Financial Institutions (Subchapter VIII of Title 26 – Financial Institutions of the Palau National Code) addressing electronic banking contains a rule that "Banks providing computer access must maintain adequate security for their Internet or proprietary platforms, including adequate systems for customer authentication and for physical and logical protection against unauthorized external access by individual penetration attempts, computer viruses, denial of service, and other forms of electronic access" (Section 10.101(d)). In addition, the Digital Residency Program has its own cybersecurity measures.[108]

Palau is a member of the Pacific Islands Law Officers' Network.[109]

106 See https://www.palaugov.pw/wp-content/uploads/Digital-Residency-Program-Cyber-Security-Regulation.pdf.
107 Promulgated by the Palau Supreme Court January 6, 2023.
108 See https://www.palaugov.pw/wp-content/uploads/Digital-Residency-Program-Cyber-Security-Regulation.pdf.
109 See https://pilonsec.org/about/members/.

5. Intellectual property and copyright

For matters of intellectual property and copyright, the primary regulation is found in Title 39, Chapter 8 of the Palau National Code Annotated. Chapter 29 of the Penal Code of the Republic of Palau specifically addresses trademark counterfeiting (Section 2906).

6. Online content regulation

The Constitution of the Republic of Palau provides several safeguards of particular relevance for online content regulation. Article IV outlines fundamental rights, including the freedom of conscience or of philosophical or religious belief (Section 1), the freedom of expression or press (s. 2), the right of any person to peacefully assemble and petition the Government for redress of grievances (s. 3), equality under the law and equal protection (s. 5), and due process (s. 6).

Chapter 49 of the Penal Code of the Republic of Palau addresses certain offences related to obscenity such as displaying indecent matter (Section 4902–4903) and promoting pornography (s. 4904–4906) that may impact online content. Similarly, the regulation of gambling in Chapter 50 may apply online.

7. Domain names

The Internet country code top-level domain for Palau is ".pw", and it is operated by PW Registry.[110]

8. Online dispute resolution

The laws of Palau do not specifically address online dispute resolution.

9. Digital ID

The Digital Residency Act of Palau introduced the Digital Residency Program in 2022 which aims to deploy digital residency IDs (DIDs) on the Solana blockchain.[111] This programme allows global citizens to obtain residency without physical presence and provides a Government-issued ID in the form of a physical card and a non-fungible token (NFT) on the blockchain, enabling legal identity and on-chain verification. The Digital Residency Act amended Chapter 10 of Title 13 of the Palau National Code and added Subchapter III, Digital Residency Program. The Act authorized the establishment of a Digital Residency Office within the Ministry of Finance to oversee and manage all activities authorized, required or allowed by the Act, including the responsibilities of service providers.

10. E-payments

E-payment is not addressed in detail. However, Chapter 10, Financial Institutions (Subchapter VIII of Title 26 – Financial Institutions of the Palau National Code), addresses electronic banking and contains a rule that "Banks may provide to their customers remote access to their accounts through computers by proprietary personal computer software or by the Internet" (Section 10.101(a)). Furthermore, s. 10.101(b) adds that "Banks that permit computer access may permit customers to transfer funds between accounts, initiate payments, and apply for credit by computer or permit any other activities for financial services a bank is not prohibited by law from offering."

Palau is in the process of launching a digital currency, which will be a stablecoin.[112] A stablecoin is a type of cryptocurrency designed to maintain a stable value by being pegged to a reserve asset, such as a fiat

110 See https://registry.pw/.
111 See https://rns.id/.
112 See https://www.palaugov.pw/wp-content/uploads/Republic-of-Palau-Stablecoin-Program-Phase-1-Report.pdf.

currency (like the United States dollar) or a commodity (like gold).

11. Taxation

The laws of Palau do not specifically address taxation of e-commerce. Important legislation includes Title 40, Revenue and Taxation of the Palau National Code. Under recent reform (from 1 January 2023), most goods and services sold or consumed in Palau are subject to 10 percent Palau Good and Services Tax (PGST).[113]

Palau is a member of the Pacific Islands Tax Administrators Association (PITAA).[114]

[113] See https://www.palaugov.pw/taxreform/pgst-registration/.
[114] See https://pitaa.org/.

I. Papua New Guinea

The legal system in Papua New Guinea is based on English common law.[115] The two main sources of law[116] are laws passed by parliament ("Statutes") and "the underlying law" – law made by judges combining principles and rules of common law and equity in England[117] as well as law derived from the customs of the various peoples of Papua New Guinea.[118]

Major change was introduced through the Digital Government Act 2022. This Act aims to "provide for digital government through the use of information and communication technologies".[119] It also seeks to "enable the streamlining, planning, coordination, development and implementation across the whole of government of digital services, digital infrastructure, digital skills and all other aspects of digital government and for related purposes."[120] The Digital Government Plan 2023–2027, mandated by the Digital Government Act 2023, outlines a flexible approach for delivering digital services, creating a resilient cyber environment and establishing digital service standards for public services.

The country's ICT Sector Roadmap indicates a shift in ICT development towards digitalization. It marks the first strategic update since the National ICT Policy 2009. The roadmap identifies six strategic pillars that form the basis of the Papua New Guinea Digital Transformation Policy 2020. The rapid pace of digital growth presents challenges in managing and protecting data. To address these risks, including data breaches and privacy violations, the National Data Governance and Data Protection Policy 2024 was introduced. The policy aims to build public trust and foster data-driven innovation.

To address the legal issues of the online environment, Papua New Guinea has introduced legislation and amended older laws in several fields. The National Information and Communications Technology Act 2009, with its extraterritorial application (Section 6), governs key aspects of the country's ICT environment.

1. E-transactions /E-signatures

The Government of Papua New Guinea developed its Electronic Transaction legislation in 2018. The Electronic Transaction Bill[121] was passed on 18 November 2021 and certified on 23 February 2022. Provisions from the United Nations Commission on International Trade Law (UNCITRAL) Model Law on Electronic Commerce (1996), the UNCITRAL Model Law on Electronic Signatures (2001), the United Nations Convention on the Use of Electronic Communications in International Contracts (2005), and the UNCITRAL Model Law on Electronic Transferable Records (2017) were all used to draft the resulting Electronic Transactions Act 2021.

2. Consumer protection

Several Acts provide consumer protection offline. The Commercial Advertisement

115 A legal information database is available at https://www.parliament.gov.pg/bills-and-legislation.
116 For a more detailed overview of the sources of law, see Section 9 of the Constitution.
117 As they stood at the time of Papua New Guinea independence on 16 September 1975.
118 Where these customs and traditions do not offend present day beliefs, Stephen Massa, Steve Patrick and Deborah Edo, Doing Business in Papua New Guinea: Overview, Thomson Reuters Practical Law, https://uk.practicallaw.thomsonreuters.com/w-007-1171?transitionType=Default&ContextData=(sc.Default)&firstPage=true)
119 Digital Government Act 2022.
120 Digital Government Act 2022.
121 See https://www.businessadvantagepng.com/wp-content/uploads/2020/06/ECOMMERCE-BILL-JUNE-2019.pdf.

(Protection of the Public) Act 1976 aims to protect the general public from "any commercial advertisement that may contain untrue, inaccurate, misleading, misrepresentative or unreasonable statements used in describing the size, quality, quantity or nature of goods or services."[122] The Goods Act 1951 outlines certain implied conditions and warranties in sale of goods situations. In addition, the Packaging Act 1974 aims to ensure that goods are properly labelled.[123] Taken together with the wide range of other Acts administered by the Independent Consumer and Competition Commission (ICCC),[124] this patchwork of instruments provides a degree of consumer protection.

The ICCC –established under the Independent Consumer and Competition Commission Act 2002– is the main economic regulator and consumer watchdog.[125] The ICCC is a member of Consumers International.[126]

Under the Independent Consumer and Competition Commission Act 2002, consumers have the right to (a) safety; (b) choice; (c) consumer education; (d) information; (e) representation; and to (f) redress (Section 105).

There are signs of reform to the consumer protection regime. A document on a "National Competition Policy" points to increased funding for the ICCC, better facilities for low-cost consumer disputes, reforms to labelling laws, an emphasis on dealing with misleading and deceptive conduct, prohibition of certain forms of conduct harmful to consumer rights, a focus on "consumer guarantees", and harmonization of laws.[127] Papua New Guinea is a member of the International Consumer Protection and Enforcement Network (ICPEN) since 2012[128] and is a founding member of the Pacific Island Network of Competition Consumer and Economic Regulators (PINCCER).[129]

3. Data protection and privacy

Section 49 of the Constitution of the Independent State of Papua New Guinea provides a right to privacy: "Every person has the right to reasonable privacy in respect of his private and family life, his communications with other persons and his personal papers and effects, except to the extent that the exercise of that right is regulated or restricted by a law that complies with Section 38 (general qualifications on qualified rights)."

To this can be added the privacy protection provided by the Protection of Private Communications Act 1973. Furthermore, Section 267 of the National Information and Communications Technology Act 2009 makes it an offence for a person engaged in supplying an ICT service to intentionally intercept a communication, use, disclose or record any communication or content sent via an ICT service or intentionally modify or interfere with any communication or content sent via an ICT service, without the consent of the person to whom the communication was sent. Furthermore, the Digital Government Act 2022 imposes certain rules of surveillance using digital technology such as static and mobile cameras, geographical positioning hardware and software, and drones (Section 32).

However, Papua New Guinea does not have any specific data protection laws.

122 See https://www.iccc.gov.pg/consumer-protection/advertising-labelling.
123 See https://www.iccc.gov.pg/consumer-protection/advertising-labelling.
124 See https://www.iccc.gov.pg/about-us/legislation/acts-administered-by-iccc.
125 See https://www.iccc.gov.pg/.
126 A membership organization bringing together over 200 member organisations in more than 100 countries to empower and champion the rights of consumers everywhere, (https://www.consumersinternational.org/who-we-are/).
127 See https://ict.gov.pg/policy/National%20Competition%20Policy.pdf.
128 See https://icpen.org/who-we-are.
129 See https://www.mted.gov.to/index.php/2023/11/07/press-release/.

Although it is a member of the Asia–Pacific Economic Commission (APEC), Papua New Guinea is yet to align itself with the APEC Privacy Framework.[130] Privacy is discussed in the Constitution and in the context of the "National Right to Information Policy". The June 2021 Consultation Paper notes that: "The [RTI Implementation Unit/Attorney-General's Office/Law Reform Commission] will be tasked with examining privacy issues and providing recommendations to ensure appropriate protections are in place and will submit a report on their findings to Parliament for consideration within [18 months] of this Policy being adopted. At that time, consideration will be given to amending this Policy and/or developing a separate policy or legislation to appropriately deal with privacy issues."[131]

Finally, it should be noted that the website for the Department of Information and Communications Technology mentions a National Data Protection Policy, and hints at possible forthcoming law and policy on the topic: "Data protection policies and legislation, which will follow this policy, are additional and separate policies and legislation that will ensure citizen data is protected both by Governments, the private sector and any other groups that uses data."[132]

4. Cybercrime and cybersecurity

Papua New Guinea has specific legislation dedicated to cybercrime, namely the Cybercrime Code Act 2016. This Act covers various offences, including hacking (s. 6), data and/or systems interference (ss. 8 and 9), data espionage (s. 10), electronic fraud and/or forgery (ss. 12 and 13), identity theft (s. 15), cyber-attacks (s. 27), as well as a range of content-related offences (discussed below in the section addressing online content regulation), and intellectual property-related offences (discussed in the section immediately below).

Criminal activities are primarily regulated by the Criminal Code Act. This includes provisions for crimes that may be committed online, such as treason (s. 37), violation of secrecy (s. 191), and obscene publications (s. 228). As amended, this Act applies in an extraterritorial manner primarily in relation to acts or omissions by a national of Papua New Guinea.[133] In 2016, via the Criminal Code (Amendment) Act 2016, the Criminal Code Act was amended to address selected online activities including incitement of unlawful unrest and riot using ICT, and unlawful publication of defamatory matters.

Procedural matters related to cybercrime are outlined in the Cybercrime Code Act 2016, which includes provisions for search and seizure (ss. 32–34), preservation of evidence (ss. 35–38), powers of investigation (ss. 39–41), evidence admissibility (ss. 42–43), the potential criminal liability of ICT service providers (ss. 44–45), and international co-operation (ss. 46-47).

Cybersecurity is articulated as a priority.[134] While elements of cybersecurity are regulated under the Cybercrime Code Act 2016, broader initiatives are guided by the National Cyber Security Policy 2021. The policy provides a strategic framework to inform cybersecurity efforts in the country, outlines the nation's objectives for protecting critical infrastructure, addresses emerging threats and fosters collaboration between Government agencies and the private sector in cybersecurity matters. Additionally, to further safeguard its digital infrastructure, Papua New Guinea has established the National Cyber Security Centre[135] and the Cyber Security Operations Centre.[136]

130 See https://www.apec.org/groups/committee-on-trade-and-investment/digital-economy-steering-group.
131 See https://ict.gov.pg/policy/Right%20to%20Informstion%20Policy%20-%20Consultation%20Paper.pdf.
132 See https://ict.gov.pg/national-data-protection-data-privacy/.
133 Criminal Code (Amendment) Act 2016.
134 See https://ict.gov.pg/cyber-security/.
135 Digital Government Act 2022, ss. 18–19.
136 See https://ict.gov.pg/1233-2/.

Although there is no standalone cybersecurity legislation, the Digital Government Act 2022 addresses critical digital infrastructure (Section 21).

Finally, other key laws include the Mutual Assistance in Criminal Matters Act 2005 and the Anti-Money Laundering and Counter Terrorist Financing Act 2015.[137] Papua New Guinea is also an active participant in international networks such as the Pacific Islands Law Officers' Network and the Global Forum on Cyber Expertise (GFCE).[138] The Government of Papua New Guinea is also making strides toward accession to the Budapest Convention on Cybercrime, with ongoing efforts to amend existing legislation to align with the convention's standards.

5. Intellectual property and copyright

Papua New Guinea law contains detailed, but partially dated, regulation of intellectual property and copyright including the Trademarks Act 1978, the Copyright and Neighboring Rights Act 2000 and the Patents and Industrial Designs Act 2000. These Acts are predominantly technology-neutral. However, the Copyright and Neighboring Rights Act 2000 specifically addresses "computer program".

Furthermore, the Cybercrime Code Act 2016 includes provisions addressing intellectual property related offences; namely online copyright infringement (s. 28), online trademark infringement (s. 29), and patent and industrial designs infringement (s. 30). Papua New Guinea is a Member State of WIPO.

6. Online content regulation

Freedom of speech and expression is established under the Constitution (Section 46). Other Constitutionally guaranteed rights of relevance online include the right to freedom of information (s. 51), the freedom of conscience, thought and religion (s. 45), as well as the freedom of assembly and association (s. 47) and the right to the full protection of the law (37(1)).

Some examples of content regulation specifically referring to electronic dissemination can be found in Papua New Guinea law. For example, via the modernizing impact of the Defamation (Amendment) Act 2016, the Defamation Act now makes specific reference to "use of electronic systems or devices" (s. 3 and s. 4). The term "public meeting" now includes "discussion forums, whether or not featured on social networking sites" (s. 8).

Further, Section 14 of the Tobacco Control Act 2016 states that "no person shall publish, or arrange for any other person to publish, any tobacco product advertisement in Papua New Guinea", and Section 2 makes clear that the term "publish" means "to disseminate by means of any other[139] electronic medium". An Internet-specific exemption for this ban can be found in Section 16(1)(c) which makes clear that the ban in Section 14 does not apply to "an Internet website for any particular seller, so long as it presents factual information about the business and does not advertise or promote tobacco products or brands."

Furthermore, the Cybercrime Code Act 2016 includes provisions addressing a range of content-related offences. Section 17 deals with pornography; Sections 18 and 19 address child pornography and child online grooming respectively; while Section 20 regulates animal pornography. The Cybercrime Code Act 2016 also addresses defamatory publication (s. 21), cyber bullying (s. 22), cyber harassment (s. 23), cyber extortion (s. 24), unlawful disclosure (s. 25), spam (s. 26) and unlawful advertising (s. 31).

To this may be added the National Information and Communications Technology Act 2009 that makes it an offence to, by means of an ICT service,

137 Combating money laundering is also a specified goal of the Companies Amendment Act 2022.
138 See https://pilonsec.org/about/members/.
139 The same provision also includes "to include in any disk for use with a computer" in the definition of "publish".

knowingly send offensive, indecent, obscene or menacing content or communications, or for the purpose of causing annoyance, inconvenience or needless anxiety to another person send any content or communication, that (s)he knows to be false; or persistently makes use of that ICT service with that intended purpose (s. 266).

7. Domain names

The Internet country code top-level domain for Papua New Guinea is ".pg", and the registry is the Department of Information Technology of the Papua New Guinea University of Technology.[140] Registration is intended for locals: "All applicants must demonstrate a local presence or interests in Papua New Guinea. Registration will not be granted if the operation is solely conducted from overseas without any local interests."[141] The Digital Government Act 2022 provides certain rules in relation to the government domain (ss. 38–40) as well as Government social media accounts (s. 41).

8. Online dispute resolution

The laws of Papua New Guinea do not specifically address online dispute resolution. However, the rules around alternative dispute resolution (ADR) may be noted.[142]

9. Digital ID

There is currently no legislation in place for regulating digital IDs. However, under the Digital Government Act 2022, a National e-Government Online Portal is due to be established (Section 35), which may prompt the adoption of some form of digital ID system.

10. E-payments

Section 28(2) of the National Payment System Act 2013 defines "electronic money" as monetary value stored electronically by an issuer upon receipt of funds, accepted as payment by parties other than the issuer. Section 28(1) specifies that only banks can issue electronic money with a license from the Central Bank. The Act also addresses "electronic transactions", defined as those conducted through electronic means. Section 26 empowers the Central Bank to issue orders and guidelines to regulate payment orders, money transfers via electronic messages, and ensure user protection in electronic payment transactions.

Finally, the Digital Government Act 2022 contains provisions relating to e-payment (see s. 35(2)(e)(iv)).

11. Taxation

Papua New Guinea does not currently have any specific e-commerce tax law. Taxation is regulated via several Acts such as the Income Tax Act 1959, the Personal Tax Act 1957, and the Goods and Services Tax Act 2003. These Acts are subject to frequent amendments, such as via the Income Tax (2021 Budget) (Amendment) Act 2020. The current tax rate for domestic suppliers of goods and services is 10 per cent. The government is revising legislation for the taxation of e-commerce with an intention to keep the same rate for e-commerce.

Papua New Guinea is a member of the OECD and Group of Twenty Inclusive Framework on Base Erosion and Profit Shifting (BEPS) project,[143] as well as the Pacific Islands Tax Administrators Association (PITAA).[144]

---

140 See https://www.unitech.ac.pg/dns.

141 See https://www.unitech.ac.pg/dns; the full domain name registration policy and the applicable domain name registration form are available from the same site.

142 See https://www.pngjudiciary.gov.pg/index.php/national-court/civil-cases/adr/adr-acts-rules; https://www.pngjudiciary.gov.pg/images/pdf/Court_Rules/2022/15_ADR-RULES-2022-FINAL.pdf.

143 See https://www.oecd.org/tax/beps/about/.

144 See https://pitaa.org/.

J. Samoa

Current laws in Samoa are a complex blend of locally made formal laws (including the Constitution, which is supreme, and parliamentary legislation), common law from formal courts, and customary law recognized by the Constitution. Additionally, English common law and equity apply as long as they are not excluded by other laws and are relevant to Samoa.[145]

The Samoa E-Commerce Strategy and Roadmap 2022 outlines a comprehensive approach to boost e-commerce adoption in Samoa. It aims to create a conducive environment for businesses and consumers to leverage online trade and focuses on seven priority areas: e-commerce readiness, ICT infrastructure, trade logistics, legal framework, electronic payments, skills development, and access to finance. The strategy includes 62 measures across these priority areas and proposes 22 strategic outputs. Priority Area 4: Legal and Regulatory Framework, focuses on the need to review existing regulatory and legal frameworks and enhance community awareness of e-commerce regulations and laws. Additionally, efforts are underway to develop a National E-commerce Policy, with the the support of the Ministry of Communications and Information Technology.

The ICT Sector Plan 2022/23-2026/27 outlines seven goals for the sector over the next five years. These include a sustainable ICT workforce and an ICT-literate population; improved domestic connectivity and access to ICT; improved e-services in priority sectors; strengthened ICT policy planning capacity and legislative and regulatory frameworks; a safe and secure ICT environment; a sustainable financing mechanism for the ICT sector with a comprehensive monitoring and evaluation framework; and effective multi-sectoral coordination and partnerships to fully leverage ICT as a tool for development.

The Samoa Digital Pathway: Digital Transformation Strategy 2023–2030 further builds on these initiatives with the the support of the Ministry of Communications and Information Technology.

1. E-transactions /E-signatures

The Samoa Electronic Transactions Act 2008 follows the UNCITRAL Model Law on Electronic Commerce (1996).[146] It addresses matters such as the legal recognition of electronic records (s. 6), requirement to be in writing (s. 7), and requirement for signature or seal (s. 8). It also covers the admissibility and evidential weight of electronic records (s. 11), the formation and validity of contracts (s. 12), and the time and place of receipt and dispatch of electronic records (s. 16).

2. Consumer protection

The Competition and Consumer Act 2016 is the primary tool for consumer protection in Samoa. It provides protection in relation to matters such as misleading or deceptive conduct (s. 55) and unfair practices (ss. 58–65). It also outlines a broad range of consumer guarantees (ss. 66–83), imposes a range of obligations on traders (ss. 84–86), and sets information and safety standards (ss. 87–91). The Act also establishes the Competition and Consumer Commission.[147]

145 Online legal information resources seem incomplete: https://www.palemene.ws/BillsActsRegulations; http://www.paclii.org/countries/ws.html.v
146 See https://samoa.tradeportal.org/media//Electronic%20Transactions%20Act%202008.pdf.
147 See https://www.mcil.gov.ws/services/consumer-protection/competition-and-consumer-protection/.

In the context of the sale of goods, consumers may also invoke the conditions and warranties provided under the Sale of Goods Act 1975. However, with the enhanced protections provided by the Competition and Consumer Act 2016, there may be few circumstances in which it makes sense for consumers to rely on the Sale of Goods Act. Notably the Competition and Consumer Act 2016 has amended the Sale of Goods Act. Section 57A was inserted, stating: "Sections 14 to 16 and 52 of this Act do not apply to a contract of sale to which Division 3 of Part 4 of the Competition and Consumer Act 2016 applies." Some sector-specific consumer protection is also provided under Part 9 of the Telecommunications Act 2005.

The Competition and Consumer Commission is a member of Consumers International.[148] Samoa is a founding member of the Pacific Island Network of Competition Consumer and Economic Regulators (PINCCER).[149]

3. Data protection and privacy

The Constitution of the Independent State of Samoa 1960 does not include a right to privacy and Samoa lacks specific data privacy legislation. Limited sector-specific data privacy protection is provided under Part 9 of the Telecommunications Act 2005.

4. Cybercrime a nd cybersecurity

In Samoa, the Crimes Act 2013 draws upon both the Budapest Convention on Cybercrime and the Commonwealth Model Law on Computer and Computer Related Crime. However, it has been noted that "Samoa is in the process of reviewing the national legislation on cybercrime and electronic evidence and expressed interest in harmonizing it with the international standards provided under the Budapest Convention."[150]

The Crimes Act 2013 has extraterritorial reach (s. 8) and covers an extensive range of cybercrimes including accessing electronic system without authorisation (s. 206); accessing electronic systems for dishonest purpose (s. 207); illegal remaining in an electronic system (s. 208); illegal interception (s. 209); damaging or interfering with electronic data (s. 210); illegal acquisition of electronic data (s. 211); illegal system interference (s. 212); illegal devices (s. 213); making, selling, distributing or possessing software for committing a crime (s. 214); identity fraud (s. 215); forgery of electronic data (s. 216); SPAM (s. 217); solicitation of children (s. 218); and harassment utilising means of electronic communication (s. 219).

In addition, the Crimes Act 2013 includes a selection of technology-neutral provisions relevant to the online environment. For example, it addresses voyeurism (s. 64), distribution or exhibition of indecent matter (s. 81), publication, distribution or exhibition of indecent material on child (s. 82), and false statement causing harm to a person's reputation (s. 117A).

The Money Laundering Prevention Act 2007 and the Mutual Assistance in Criminal Matters Act 2007 are also of note. Beyond the items mentioned above, Samoan law does not address cybersecurity.

Samoa is a member of the Pacific Islands Law Officers' Network.[151]

148 A membership organization bringing together over 200 member organisations in more than 100 countries to empower and champion the rights of consumers everywhere: https://www.consumersinternational.org/who-we-are/.

149 See https://www.mted.gov.to/index.php/2023/11/07/press-release/.

150 See https://www.coe.int/en/web/octopus/-/samoa?redirect=https://www.coe.int/en/web/octopus/country-wiki?p_p_id=101_INSTANCE_AZnxfNT8Y3ZI&p_p_lifecycle=0&p_p_state=normal&p_p_mode=view&p_p_col_id=column-4&p_p_col_pos=1&p_p_col_count=2.

151 See https://pilonsec.org/about/members/.

5. Intellectual property and copyright

The law of Samoa addresses intellectual property and copyright in a technology-neutral manner. Key legislation includes the Copyright Act 1998, and the Intellectual Property Act 2011.[152] The latter specifically includes "electronic mail, telex, telegrams and any other electronically produced means of communication" in its definition of "in writing" (Section 2). Additionally, the Copyright Act 1998 specifically addresses works in electronic form (s. 28).

Samoa is a Member State of WIPO and has acceded to the Berne Convention for the Protection of Literary and Artistic Works.

6. Online content regulation

The Constitution of the Independent State of Samoa 1960 guarantees freedom of speech and expression (Section 13(a)). Other Constitutionally guaranteed rights of particular relevance online include the right to freedom of religion (s. 11), freedom of assembly and association (s. 13(b and c)), and protection from discrimination (s. 15).

In Samoa, certain Acts contain sections that specifically regulate online content. For example, Section 88A of the Casino and Gambling Control Act 2010 addresses interactive gaming, and Part 9 of the Gaming Control Act 2017 regulates gaming activities by telecommunication service providers. Similarly, as amended, the Indecent Publications Ordinance 1960 now also covers indecent documents in the form of an electronic device (Section 2). The Media Council Act 2015 aims to promote professional journalism and integrity in the news media, while observing the fundamental rights under Part II of the Constitution. This Act, when referring to the term "publication" means "the dissemination to the public of any written, digital, audio or video material, and includes any material disseminated through the Internet." (s. 2).

Other Acts –such as the Defamation Act 1993 and the Alcohol Control Act 2020 (see in particular Section 52 relating to controls over the advertising and promotion of alcohol)– are largely technology-neutral and may presumably apply also to online content.

7. Domain names

The country code top level domain for Samoa is ".ws", and the registry is Samoa NIC.[153] The applicable dispute policy is available on the registry's website.[154]

8. Online dispute resolution

With its Arbitration Act dating back to 1976 and its Alternative Dispute Resolution Act 2007, Samoa seemingly has an established culture of alternative dispute resolution. While specific regulations for online dispute resolution are lacking, the definition of a "mediation session" in the latter Act includes "a meeting conducted by telephone, video conferencing or any other electronic means" (Section 2).

9. Digital ID

The National Digital Identification Act of Samoa was passed in 2024 to establish the country's first-ever digital ID system and modernize its civil registration system. This initiative, supported by the World Bank, is part of a broader effort to enhance financial inclusion and digital services for the population. The digital ID system is set to be operational by 2025.

152 Amended via the Intellectual Property Amendment Act 2020 to give effect to the Patent Cooperation Treaty, the Geneva Act (1999) of the Hague Agreement Concerning the International Registration of Industrial Designs, and the Geneva Act of the Lisbon Agreement on Appellations of Origin and Geographical Indications.

153 See https://samoanic.ws/.

154 See https://www.samoanic.ws/faq/questions_dispute.dhtml.

10. E-payments

Under Section 38 of the Central Bank of Samoa Act 2015, the Central Bank has the sole right of issuing currency in Samoa. The National Payment System Act 2014 paves the way for the issuance of electronic money (Section 40).[155]

11. Taxation

Samoa does not currently have any e-commerce specific tax law, and taxation is regulated via several Acts, such as the Value-Added Goods and Services Tax Act 2015, the Tax Administration Act 2012, and the Income Tax Act 2012. However, via the Tax Administration (Electronic System) Amendment Act 2020, the "IRS may implement electronic systems to obtain and monitor accurate records relating to the imposition of a tax."[156]

Samoa is a member of the OECD Group of Twenty Inclusive Framework on Base Erosion and Profit Shifting (BEPS) project[157] and of the Pacific Islands Tax Administrators Association (PITAA).[158]

155 Resulting in services such as: https://mycash.ws/.
156 See https://www.palemene.ws/wp-content/uploads/Tax-Administration-Electronic-System-Amendment-Act-2020-Eng.pdf.
157 See https://www.oecd.org/tax/beps/about/.
158 See https://pitaa.org/.

K. Solomon Islands

The Constitution is the supreme law of Solomon Islands, and any laws that conflict with it are considered invalid. The Constitution empowers the Parliament to legislate for "peace, order, and good government." Parliamentary Acts of the United Kingdom effective from 1 January 1961 were adopted by the Constitution, subject to national laws. Customary law, as defined in Article 144(1), ranks next in the legal hierarchy and includes local customary rules. Common law and equity principles are recognized by the Constitution but only apply when they do not conflict with the Constitution, national laws, or customary law, and when appropriate for local circumstances.[159]

The Government of Solomon Islands launched its first-ever National E-commerce Strategy (NECS) in July 2023. It was developed by the Ministries of Commerce, Industry, Labour and Immigration (MCILI) and the Ministry of Communication and Aviation (MCA). Recommendations outlined in the strategy suggest enacting legislation on e-transactions and e-signatures, guided by UNCITRAL model laws. Recommendations also include updating the 1995 Consumer Protection Act along with related subordinate legislation to align with United Nations guidelines and incorporate public input. Additionally the strategy recommends finalizing and adopting the National Cybersecurity Policy Draft and the Draft Cybercrime Regulation after thorough review. There is a call to establish a comprehensive data privacy and protection law that addresses personal and enterprise data, including national and cross-border data transfers. Finally, the strategy proposes that market analysis should be conducted to evaluate the impact of e-commerce, which may require adjustments to the existing Intellectual Property Rights (Copyright) Act, Competition Law, and other key regulations.

The Central Bank of Solomon Islands (CBSI) adopted the National Financial Inclusion Strategy 3 (2021–2025) and signed a Memorandum of Understanding with the Telecommunications Commission of Solomon Islands (TCSI) in 2022 to improve digital and mobile services collaboration. A nationwide mobile money service was launched in 2023 which is expected to bolster the fintech landscape. In addition, Solomon Islands Government ICT Services adopted a five-year ICT Strategic Plan in 2019 to enhance the Government's ICT capabilities.

1. E-transactions /E-signatures

Solomon Islands has not adopted any legislation on e-transactions or e-signatures.[160]

2. Consumer protection

The Solomon Islands Consumer Protection Act (Cap. 63) is designed to protect "the rights and interests of the consumer" and establish "certain standards of conduct by those engaged in the production, sale and distribution of goods and services to consumers" (Section 4(1)). In the pursuit of these objectives, the Act establishes a Consumer Affairs Division (s. 5(1)).[161] The Act

159 A legal information database is available at https://www.parliament.gov.sb/acts-parliament. Note the Legislation Act 2023 (https://www.parliament.gov.sb/sites/default/files/2023-12/Legislation%20Act%202023.pdf).

160 Note some databases indicate that Solomon Islands has e-transactions laws. However, they appear to refer to the Secured Transaction Act No.4/2008 which is not a good fit for that description. See for example https://unctad.org/page/cyberlaw-tracker-country-detail?country=sb.

161 See https://www.commerce.gov.sb/departments-units/consumer-affairs-and-price-control.html.

contains several mechanisms for consumer protection. For example, Section 12 opens the possibility of prescribed product safety or quality standard, Section 24 addresses misleading or deceptive conduct, Section 25 deals with false representations, Section 28 provides certain warranties in relation to the supply of services, and Section 17 makes the refusal to sell goods an offence.

Some sector-specific consumer protection is also provided under Part 11 of the Telecommunications Act (Cap. 115),[162] and under the Payment Systems Act 2022, in particular Part 10.[163] Finally, Solomon Islands is a founding member of the Pacific Island Network of Competition Consumer and Economic Regulators (PINCCER).[164]

3. Data protection and privacy

Solomon Islands lacks specific data privacy laws. The Constitution's discussion of privacy is limited to "the search of his person or his property or the entry by others on his premises." (Constitution, Section 9(1)). Some sector-specific data privacy protection is provided under Part 11 of the Telecommunications Act (Cap. 115).[165] The Tax Administration Act 2022 contains rules regarding information collection and handling in its specific context (ss. 94–106).

4. Cybercrime and cybersecurity

Solomon Islands has a draft cybercrime regulation. Some relevant offences are outlined in Part 17 of the Telecommunications Act (Cap. 115).[166] In particular, Section 120 regulates matters such as intercepting transmissions, damaging, deleting, altering or supressing telecommunications data, and revealing contents of messages. Furthermore, as discussed below, the Penal Code (Cap. 26) contains certain offences relevant to the online environment.

In terms of cybersecurity, the National Cybersecurity Policy, launched on 20 August 2024, articulates a vision of a safe, secure and robust cybersecurity environment that supports economic growth and social development. The policy builds upon existing frameworks including the National ICT Policy and National Security Strategy, and sets seven cybersecurity objectives. These include protecting critical infrastructure, creating a robust legal framework and enhancing national capacity to manage incidents. The policy emphasizes a collaborative, multi-stakeholder approach involving Government, the private sector and international partnerships, to address evolving cyber threats.

The Solomon Islands Cybersecurity Working Group (SICWG) has been established to oversee policy implementation, while the planned Solomon Islands CERT (SICERT) will manage incident reporting and response, raise awareness, and support critical infrastructure providers.

Furthermore, the technology-neutral Official Secrets Act (Cap. 25) contains provisions that may be of relevance to an online context. For example, under Section 4(c), it is a felony if a person "obtains, collects, records, or publishes, or communicates to any other person any secret official code word, or pass word, or any sketch, plan, model, article, or note, or other document or information which is calculated to be, or might be, or is intended to be, directly or indirectly useful to an enemy" if doing so "for any purpose prejudicial to the safety or interests of the State". Solomon Islands is a member of the Pacific Islands Law Officers' Network.[167]

162 See https://www.parliament.gov.sb/files/legislation/Acts/Telecommunications_Act%202009.pdf.
163 See https://www.cbsi.com.sb/wp-content/uploads/2023/04/Payment-Systems-Act-2022.pdf.
164 See https://www.mted.gov.to/index.php/2023/11/07/press-release/.
165 See https://www.parliament.gov.sb/files/legislation/Acts/Telecommunications_Act%202009.pdf.
166 See https://www.parliament.gov.sb/files/legislation/Acts/Telecommunications_Act%202009.pdf.
167 See https://pilonsec.org/about/members/.

5. Intellectual property and copyright

The primary legislative instruments for intellectual property and copyright in Solomon Islands include the Copyright Act (Cap. 138), which entered into force in 1988; the Registration of United Kingdom Patents Act (Cap. 179); the Registration of United Kingdom Trade Marks Act (Cap. 180); and the United Kingdom Designs (Protection) Act (Cap. 181). Solomon Islands is a Member State of WIPO and has acceded to the Berne Convention for the Protection of Literary and Artistic Works.

The IP strategy for Solomon Islands, launched in 2016, outlines key recommendations to modernize and enhance the intellectual property framework. The strategy highlights the need to review the current Copyright Act (Cap. 138) and establish comprehensive intellectual property legislation tailored to the nation's developmental goals and international commitments. This review would address gaps in the protection of copyright and related rights, particularly in the context of digitalization and the evolving creative industries.

Work is ongoing to implement these recommendations, including legislative updates and institutional capacity-building. These efforts are expected to create a more robust and accessible IP system, offering greater support for local creators, traditional knowledge holders and businesses seeking to protect their innovations and cultural assets both domestically and internationally.

6. Online content regulation

Freedom of expression is established under the Constitution (s. 12). Other Constitutionally guaranteed rights of particular relevance online include the right to freedom of conscience (including freedom of thought and of religion, freedom to change his religion or belief, and freedom, either alone or in community with others, and both in public and in private, to manifest and propagate his religion or belief in worship, teaching, practice and observance) (s. 11), as well as the freedom of assembly and association (s. 13), protection from discrimination (s. 15) and the right to the secure protection of law (s. 10).

The Sedition Act (Cap. 32) may be relevant for online content regulation. Although primarily focused on hard copies, it cannot be ruled out that it may apply also in an online context. Additionally, as noted above, the Penal Code (Cap. 26), which has extraterritorial reach (s. 6), includes offences that may be relevant to the online environment. These include trafficking in obscene publications (s. 173), criminal defamation (ss. 191–198), and pretending to tell fortunes (s. 310) all of which appear to be framed in a technology-neutral manner.

7. Domain names

The Internet country code top-level domain for Solomon Islands is ".sb". Section 84 of the Telecommunications Act (Cap. 115)[168] makes clear that the Telecommunications Commission has overriding responsibility for the domain. Currently, the domain is administered by the Council of Country Code Administrators.[169]

8. Online dispute resolution

The laws of Solomon Islands do not specifically address online dispute resolution.

9. Digital ID

The laws of Solomon Islands do not specifically address digital ID. A cabinet paper has been submitted proposing work on a national ID system to establish

168 See https://www.parliament.gov.sb/files/legislation/Acts/Telecommunications_Act%202009.pdf.
169 See https://cocca.org.nz/.

a foundational framework for identity management. There has been no significant progress on this initiative to date, leaving the development and implementation of a digital ID system as an unaddressed gap in the country's digital infrastructure.

10. E-payments

The laws of Solomon Islands do not specifically address e-payment. Under Section 25(1) of the Central Bank of Solomon Islands Act 2012, "The Central Bank shall have the sole right of issuing currency notes and coins for, on behalf of and throughout Solomon Islands, and no other persons shall issue currency notes, bank notes or coins or any documents or tokens payable to bearer on demand being documents or tokens having the appearance of currency notes or coins."

Finally, the Payment Systems Act 2022 must be noted[170] as it contains specific rules regarding electronic banking and funds transfer (Part 9).

11. Taxation

The laws of Solomon Islands do not specifically address taxation of e-commerce. However, the Tax Administration Act 2022 contains specific provisions regarding electronic documents in the context of an electronic tax system (ss. 164–167). Other important legislation includes the Sales Tax Act (Cap. 125), the Income Tax Act (Cap. 123), and the Goods Tax Act (Cap. 122). Note also the Value Added Tax Bill 2023.[171] Solomon Islands is a member of the Pacific Islands Tax Administrators Association (PITAA).[172]

170 See https://www.cbsi.com.sb/wp-content/uploads/2023/04/Payment-Systems-Act-2022.pdf.
171 See https://www.parliament.gov.sb/sites/default/files/2023-09/Value%20Added%20Tax%20Bill%202023.pdf.
172 See https://pitaa.org/.

L. Timor-Leste

In Timor-Leste, legitimate sources of law include the Constitution of the Republic, laws issued by the National Parliament and the Government, as well as the regulations and other legislative instruments established by the United Nations Transitional Administration in East Timor (UNTAET). Indonesian laws, provided they have not been repealed, continue to supplement these sources of law. Additionally, international law and customary law are applied in certain contexts.[173]

Digital transformation in Timor-Leste is underscored by a ten-year strategic plan, Timor Digital 2032. This envisions the integration of digital technologies and ICT across key areas such as e-Government, the inclusive economy, health, education and agriculture. The plan is designed to be adaptable and will progressively include additional areas based on Government priorities. Current objectives include delivering Government services through digital means, fostering an inclusive economy and strengthening the health, education, and agriculture sectors. The plan aims to create an enabling environment for digital technology development and advance e-commerce.

The eTrade Readiness Assessment, conducted by UN Trade and Development in 2023 in cooperation with the Government of Timor-Leste, highlighted key gaps and opportunities within the e-commerce ecosystem. Following this, Timor-Leste is currently developing its National E-commerce Strategy (2025–2029) which aims to establish e-commerce as a key driver of economic development by enhancing access to digital markets and empowering MSMEs.

1. E-transactions /E-signatures

Decree-Law No. 12/2024, effective 18 August 2024, aligns with Timor Digital 2032 and addresses the need to facilitate electronic interactions between the public and private sectors. It aims to promote economic growth and innovation, will remain technology-neutral and align with international standards for e-commerce and electronic signatures. In more detail, the Decree-Law incorporates the UNCITRAL Model Law on Electronic Commerce (1996), the UNCITRAL Model Law on Electronic Signatures (2001), the United Nations Convention on the Use of Electronic Communications in International Contracts (2005), and the UNCITRAL Model Law on Electronic Transferable Records (2017).

This new law applies to all individuals or entities engaging in e-commerce with those domiciled or established in Timor-Leste, covering electronic records, signatures, and contract formation, while excluding specific acts like wills, family law matters, and certain real estate and judicial documents.
It ensures the legal effectiveness of electronic records and signatures, setting conditions for their preservation and use as legal evidence. The law designates the Agency for Information and Communication Technologies (TIC TIMOR) as the accrediting authority for certifying entities for electronic signatures, outlining their responsibilities for security and reliability, and allowing certificates from equivalent foreign entities. Additionally, it prohibits unsolicited commercial electronic messages (spam) without a functional return address or objection mechanism and establishes a sanctioning regime with fines ranging from $500 to $100,000 for administrative offences.

[173] Online legal information resources seem incomplete: https://mj.gov.tl/jornal/lawsTL/RDTL-Law/index-e.htm; http://www.worldlii.org/tp/legis/decree_law/; http://timor-leste.gov.tl/?lang=en#.

2. Consumer protection

Research identified a Consumer Protection law (LAW No. 8/2016 of 8 July).[174] Further, sectoral consumer protection is catered for in Section 20 of the Decree-Law No. 11/2003 of 29 July, Establishing the Bases for the Telecommunications Sector. This requires that: "Consumers have the right to use public telecommunications services with the service quality as required by the applicable legal and regulatory provisions."

3. Data protection and privacy

A Data Privacy and Protection Law has been drafted as of 2021, but further information is not available.

Chapter V of the Penal Code (approved by Decree-Law No. 19/2009) addresses violations of privacy. Article 183 deals with the public disclosure of private information, Article 184 addresses breaches of secrecy, and Article 187 addresses tampering with correspondence or telecommunications. For all these matters, prosecutions depend on a complaint being filed. Further, aspects of privacy are protected under Law No. 10/2011 of 14 September which enacted the Civil Code. Article 67 provides general protection of personality, while Article 76 protects the right to an image and Article 77 safeguards the intimacy of private life.

In addition, a degree of data privacy is also catered for under Section 18 of the Decree-Law No. 11/2003 of 29 July Establishing the Bases for the Telecommunications Sector that ensures that the "secrecy of communications transmitted through the public telecommunications networks is guaranteed, except in cases contemplated by law on matters of criminal investigation and national security." Furthermore, some limited sectoral rules with privacy implications may be found. For example, Article 17 of the Customs Code Decree Law No.14 (2017) deals with confidentiality duty imposed on customs officials. Further, Article 85(3) requires that: "Access to personal data or data from organizations involved in customs activities shall be restricted to duly authorized customs officials."

Finally, in the context of data privacy it may also be noted that Law No. 2/2010 of 21 April, Law on National Security emphasizes the need to respect human rights. For example, Article 4(4) states: "In defending its sovereignty, the State respects human rights and the rights of peoples, the fundamental rights, liberties and guarantees of national and foreign citizens."[175]

4. Cybercrime and cybersecurity

In June 2020 a draft Criminal Defamation Law was proposed and a draft Cybercrime Law was proposed in January 2021.

The Penal Code (approved by Decree-Law No. 19/2009) –with limited extraterritorial reach (Article 8)– contains provisions specifically addressing the online environment. Article 268 deals with computer fraud, and Article 269 covers aggravated online fraud. Other provisions –such as Article 313 on money laundering[176] and Article 285 regulating defamatory false information– clearly apply to online activity due to their technology-neutral wording such as "by any means" in the case of Article 285.

A degree of cybersecurity regulation is provided by Section 23(1)(d) of Decree-Law No. 11/2003 of 29 July Establishing the Bases for the Telecommunications Sector, which regulates the wilful modification or interference with the tenor of any communication sent through the public telecommunications network. Additional

[174] See http://timor-leste.gov.tl/wp-content/uploads/2021/03/Lei_de_PRotecao_ao_Consumidor2.pdf.

[175] See also Law No. 2/2010 of 21 April Law on National Security, Article 39(5).

[176] See also Law No. 17/2011 of 28th of December Legal Regime Covering the Prevention of and Combat Against Money Laundering and Financing of Terrorism.

emphasis on cybersecurity is found in Article 40 of Law No. 2/2010 of 21 April, Law on National Security, with its specific reference to the security of information and IT systems.[177] Further, regarding cybersecurity, Article 85(3) of the Customs Code Decree Law No.14 (2017), as noted in the earlier context of data privacy, is also relevant.

In 2022, Timor-Leste was invited to join the Council of Europe Convention on Cybercrime.[178] Work to bring the domestic legal framework of Timor-Leste in line with the provisions of the treaty is underway.[179]

5. Intellectual property and copyright

Examples of laws with an impact on intellectual property and copyright can be found in Law No. 2/2007 on National Symbols[180] and the Code of Business Registration (approved by Decree-Law No. 7/2006 of 1 March 2006).[181] Article 184 of the Penal Code (approved by Decree-Law No. 19/2009) applies to breaches of secrecy and provides a means to protect trade secrets in the context of intellectual property. Research indicates that Law No. 14/2022, dated December 22, has introduced a Copyright and Related Rights Code,[182] which establishes a more comprehensive framework for regulating intellectual property and copyright. Finally, it must be noted that the Constitution also protects intellectual property. Article 60 states that: "The State shall guarantee and protect the creation, production and commercialization of literary, scientific and artistic work, including the legal protection of copyrights."

6. Online content regulation

The Constitution protects the right to freedom of speech and the right to inform and be informed impartially (Section 40(1)) and makes clear that these rights "shall not be limited by any sort of censorship" (s.40(2)). Nevertheless, exercising these rights "shall be regulated by law based on the imperative of respect for the Constitution and the dignity of the human person" (s.40(3)). Other notable Constitutional guarantees in the context of online content regulation include freedom of the press and mass media (s. 41), freedom of conscience, religion and worship (s. 45), and the right to political participation (s. 46),

The Penal Code (approved by Decree-Law No. 19/2009) impacts certain forms of online content beyond those already discussed above. For example, Article 131(2) makes it a crime to promote a terrorist group, organization or association, and Article 134(1) criminalizes the incitement of hatred against a race, people or nation, with the intention to provoke war or prevent peaceful fellowship among different races, peoples or nations. Similarly, Article 135(1) addresses organized propaganda inciting or encouraging religious or racial discrimination, hatred or violence, and Article 200 deals with breaches of State secrets. Furthermore, Article 144(1) makes it a crime to incite another person to commit suicide, or provide assistance for said purpose, if the suicide is actually attempted or consummated. Article 176 addresses child pornography.

177 See also Law No. 9/2008 on the Intelligence System of the Democratic Republic of Timor-Leste.
178 See https://www.coe.int/en/web/cybercrime/-/timor-leste-invited-to-join-the-convention-on-cybercrime.
179 See https://www.coe.int/en/web/cybercrime/-/glacy-co-operation-with-timor-leste-on-the-legislative-reform-on-cybercrime-and-electronic-evidence.
180 See https://www.wipo.int/wipolex/en/text/244546.
181 See https://www.wipo.int/wipolex/en/text/243220.
182 See https://mj.gov.tl/jornal/public/docs/2022/serie_1/SERIE_I_NO_51_A.pdf.

Law No. 10/2011 of 14 September, which approves the Civil Code also contains provisions affecting online content. For example, Article 418 covers defamation: "Any person who makes or disseminates a statement liable to harm the personal standing or good name of any natural or legal person shall be liable for the damage caused."

Finally, Section 21 of the Decree-Law No. 11/2003 of 29 July, Establishing the Bases for the Telecommunications Sector ensures that "Telecommunications that involve disregard for the laws or undermine the state security, public order or social mores are prohibited."

7. Domain names

The Internet country code top-level domain for Timor-Leste is ".tl". Currently, the domain is administered by the Council of Country Code Administrators.[183]

8. Online dispute resolution

The laws of Timor-Leste do not specifically address online dispute resolution. However, as the country works toward deeper integration with the Association of Southeast Asian Nations (ASEAN) and its membership aspirations, developing online dispute resolution mechanisms will be critical to align with the region's e-commerce policies. The ASEAN Economic Community Blueprint 2025 emphasizes the need for a harmonized legal framework for online dispute resolution to support cross-border e-commerce transactions.

Timor-Leste is committed to upgrading its e-commerce ecosystem, as seen in its ongoing National E-commerce Strategy. This indicates that adopting online dispute resolution mechanisms will likely become part of its legal framework. This would align with ASEAN efforts to harmonize consumer protection laws and implement secure, user-friendly electronic identification mechanisms that enhance the reliability of online transactions.

9. Digital ID

Although the current legal framework of Timor-Leste does not specifically address digital ID, the Government, with support from the Asian Development Bank (ADB), is working on implementing a Unique Identity (UID) System. This will provide citizens, residents and even foreigners with a digital identity using a unique number, biographical data, and biometric information. The project aims to create a single, reliable digital identity and resolve the issue of multiple ID systems across various Government agencies. The UID will play a crucial role in enhancing digital authentication and improving the security of digital transactions, particularly for e-commerce.

10. E-payments

Timor-Leste has yet to adopt comprehensive legislation for e-payments. While the Central Bank of Timor-Leste has established systems such as R-Timor and P24 to facilitate interbank payments, further regulatory updates are required to fully address the rise of e-payments and digital financial services.

11. Taxation

The main legislation for taxation is the Taxes and Duties Act (Law No. 8/2008 of 30 June 2008).[184] Timor-Leste is a member of the Pacific Islands Tax Administrators Association (PITAA).[185]

183 See https://cocca.org.nz/.
184 See https://www.wipo.int/wipolex/en/text/244563.
185 See https://pitaa.org/.

M. Tonga

The Kingdom of Tonga is a constitutional monarchy. Sources of law include the Constitution, local legislation, colonial legislation, specific English Acts of Parliament applicable to Tonga, and common law and equity.[186]

Tonga has made notable progress in strengthening its digital economy framework, guided by the National ICT Policy and the E-Commerce Strategy and Roadmap (2021). The roadmap, under Priority Area 4: Legal and Regulatory Framework, highlights the need for a comprehensive review of the existing e-commerce regulatory and legal framework to ensure alignment with international standards. It also emphasizes the importance of raising community awareness about e-commerce regulations and laws, as well as ensuring their effective enforcement. Additionally, the 2019–2024 Digital Government Strategic Framework aims to deepen the use of ICT within Government agencies, with specific objectives for expanding digital platforms in public education and other services.

The regulatory landscape for e-commerce in Tonga is also evolving, led by the Digital Transformation Department. Ongoing legislative efforts include the Data Protection and Privacy Bill, the Cybersecurity Bill and the Cybercrimes Bill. These initiatives are crucial for establishing a secure digital environment and protecting user data, positioning Tonga alongside international cybersecurity norms. The Cyber Challenges Task Force (CCTF), established on 13 December 2013, remains a cornerstone in addressing cybersecurity challenges. This task force, which is a collaborative effort between the Government, non-governmental organizations, the private sector and development partners, provides a coordinated response to technological issues, reflecting the commitment by Tonga to tackling cybersecurity threats.[187]

1. E-transactions /E-signatures

Tonga currently lacks laws governing e-transactions and e-signature laws. Work on an Electronic Transactions Act is still ongoing. This will establish the legal framework for the recognition of electronic contracts and digital signatures, an essential foundation for a robust e-commerce system.

2. Consumer protection

In Tonga, the technology-neutral Consumer Protection Act (Cap. 17.04) is the main instrument protecting consumers online and offline. It includes provisions regulating matters such as approved standards (ss. 12–14), product recalls (s. 16), misleading or deceptive conduct (s. 22), false representations (s. 23), and warranties in relation to the supply of services (s. 26). The Consumer Protection Act also establishes a Consumer Affairs Division (s. 4).

In addition, the Consumer Protection (Product Safety and Labelling Standards) Regulations imposes certain safety and labelling standards, and the Food Act (Cap 19.03) specifically addresses food labelling and standards, as well as safety of imported and exported food. Sector-specific consumer protection can also be found under Part VII of the Communications Act (Cap. 15.01). In 2022, a Draft National Policy on Consumer Protection and Competition was initiated by the Ministry of Trade and Economic Development. As result of this work, a review of the Consumer Protection Act is currently underway.

Tonga is a founding member of the Pacific Island Network of Competition Consumer and Economic Regulators (PINCCER).[188]

186 Online legal information resources seem incomplete: https://ago.gov.to/cms/; http://www.paclii.org/countries/to.html
187 See https://www.coe.int/en/web/octopus/-/tonga.
188 See https://www.mted.gov.to/index.php/2023/11/07/press-release/.

3. Data protection and privacy

Some Tongan laws provide issue-specific privacy protections, such as the Mental Health Act, the Education Act, Tonga Police Act and Anti-Corruption Commissioner Act. The same can be said of Section 25 of the Banking Act 2020, which sets rules for confidentiality.

While Tonga lacks a comprehensive data protection law, and its Constitution (Cap. 1.01) does not mention privacy, a Privacy Bill has been in development since 2018 under a Cabinet Directive, with Cabinet granting approval to proceed in 2022. This will fill the legislative gap by providing comprehensive protections for personal data, particularly in e-commerce.

4. Cybercrime and cybersecurity

The Computer Crimes Act 2019 (Cap. 4.02) has extraterritorial reach (Section 3) and provides detailed rules on issues such as illegal access (s. 4), interference with data (s. 5), interference with computer system (s. 6), illegal interception of data (s. 7), illegal devices (s. 8), and a range of procedural powers (ss. 9–16). As the Act was first introduced in 2003, a separate Bill (the Computer Crimes Bill 2019[189]) was tabled to update these provisions but was later withdrawn from Parliament.

The Electronic Communication Abuse Offences Act 2020 has extraterritorial reach (s. 3(b)) and addresses "bullying, menacing, harassing, harmful, indecent, and such other material which in the determination of the Court would cause harm to a reasonable person in that person's situation." (s. 2(1)). In addition, the Criminal Offences Act (Cap. 4.02) contains provisions that may be relevant online. This Act addresses sedition (s. 47), and child pornography (s. 115A). Refer also to the Mutual Assistance in Criminal Matters Act 2000 and the Money Laundering and Proceeds of Crime Act 2000. Tonga is a member of the Pacific Islands Law Officers' Network.[190]

Tonga lacks specific cybersecurity laws beyond the provisions discussed above. However, in July 2016, Tonga launched its first CERT team. Known as CERT.to, the team is attached to the Information and ICT department of the Ministry of Meteorology, Energy, Information, Disaster Management, Climate Change and Communications.[191] In May 2022, the Government approved the drafting and preparation of a Cybersecurity Bill for further review. Tonga is a party to the Convention on Cybercrime of the Council of Europe (CETS No.185), commonly known as the Budapest Convention.[192]

5. Intellectual property and copyright

The Copyright Act (Cap. 17.05) contains both technology-neutral and technology-specific provisions relevant to e-commerce. An example is found in Section 14, relating to the reproduction and adaptation of computer programmes. Other relevant legislation includes the Industrial Property Act (Cap. 17.07), the Protection of Geographical Indications Act 2002 (Act No. 17 of 2002, 2020 Revised Edition), and the Protection of Layout Designs (Topographies) of Integrated Circuits Act (Cap. 17.13). Tonga is a Member State of WIPO and has acceded to the Berne Convention for the Protection of Literary and Artistic Works.

6. Online content regulation

Freedom of speech and of the press is established under the Constitution (s. 7(1)). Other Constitutionally guaranteed rights of particular relevance online include the right to freedom of worship (s. 5), as well as the equality before the law (s. 4).

189 See https://ago.gov.to/cms/images/LEGISLATION/BILLS/2019/2019-0025/ComputerCrimesBill2019.pdf.
190 See https://pilonsec.org/about/members/.
191 See https://www.coe.int/en/web/octopus/-/tonga
192 See https://www.coe.int/en/web/conventions/full-list?module=treaty-detail&treatynum=185.

Under Part 3 of The Electronic Communication Abuse Offences Act 2020, victims of certain activities may pursue civil proceedings against a defendant in court. It is worth noting that this Act has far-reaching implications for third parties, such as service providers. For example, under Section 9(2): "A stop publication order may be made against a respondent, service provider or relevant party, even if they did not know or have reason to believe that the electronic communication is an abuse under this Act." Part 5 of the Act outlines a range of service provider obligations.

Part IX, Division 2 of the of the Communications Act (Cap. 15.01) contains detailed rules relating to matters such as take-down notices (Section 106), opt-out filtering (s. 107), mandatory filtering (s. 108), and Internet service providers' duty to report child pornography (s. 109). Part XI, Division 3 of the same Act provides safe harbour protection for access service providers (s. 173), hosting service providers (s. 174), caching service providers (s. 175), and persons who link end users to computer data provided by a third person (s. 176), in certain situations.

7. Domain names

The Tongan Internet Corporation Register Act (Cap. 15.07) establishes the Tongan Internet Corporation Register, which operates under the oversight of the Minister responsible for telecommunications. Registration is also open to foreign persons, corporations and statutory bodies formed under foreign law (s. 3(2)).[193] Fees for registration are outlined in the Tongan Internet Corporation Register (Fees) Regulations.

The Internet country code top-level-domain for Tonga is ".to". Section 69 of the Communications Act (Cap. 15.01) regulates responsibility for electronic addressing, including the registration and allocation of domain names. Under this provision, the Minister or their nominated representatives are responsible for electronic addressing. The Tonga Network Information Center is the registry for the ".to" ccTLD.[194]

8. Online dispute resolution

Tonga has taken steps to encourage dispute resolution outside the court system, for example in the form of the International Arbitration Act 2020. However, Tonga lacks specific online dispute resolution rules.

9. Digital ID

The laws of Tonga do not specifically address digital ID. However, at the time of writing, Tonga is working on developing and implementing its e-identification (eID) system as part of its digital transformation and e-governance strategy.

10. E-payments

The laws of Tonga do not specifically address e-payment. However, efforts are underway to develop an E-Payment Bill with support from the Pacific Agreement on Closer Economic Relations (PACER Plus) and the National Reserve Bank of Tonga. This initiative builds on the launch of the Domestic Electronic Payment System in 2022, which modernized payment infrastructure by enabling efficient and secure electronic transactions.

11. Taxation

The laws of Tonga do not specifically address taxation of e-commerce. However, existing legislation does include the Consumption Tax Act (Cap. 11.01), and the Income Tax Act (Cap. 11.05).

Tonga is a member of the Pacific Islands Tax Administrators Association (PITAA).[195]

[193] See also the Communications Act (Cap. 15.01), Part VI, Division 3.
[194] See https://www.tonic.to/.
[195] See https://pitaa.org/.

N. Tuvalu

The legal framework of Tuvalu comprises the Constitution, Acts of Parliament, English common law and equity, pre-Independence British Acts still in effect, and customary laws. Customary laws apply in matters such as land title and civil or criminal cases in magistrates' courts. However, they must not contradict principles of natural justice, equity, or current laws, except where these are inconsistent with the Constitution or other legislation. A Constitution of Tuvalu Bill was presented in 2022.[196] As is made clear in the Laws of Tuvalu Act (Cap. 1.06), in addition to the Constitution, the laws of Tuvalu comprise every Act, customary law, the common law of Tuvalu, and every applied law (Section 4).[197]

The 2021 Tuvalu National ICT Policy outlines the country's strategic framework for developing and utilizing ICT. Proposed legal developments include establishing a supportive environment through universal access to ICT; online transactions and data security; implementing policies that ensure open, non-discriminatory access and protect privacy; and addressing cybercrime and online child exploitation while aligning ICT regulations with international and national laws and standards.

1. E-transactions /E-signatures

The laws of Tuvalu do not specifically address e-transactions and e-signatures. Work on an Electronic Transactions Act is ongoing. Tuvalu is a party to the United Nations Convention on the Use of Electronic Communications in International Contracts (New York, 2005), and this treaty entered into force during 2023. Tuvalu has also acceded to the United Nations Framework Agreement on Facilitation of Cross-border Paperless Trade in Asia and the Pacific.[198]

2. Consumer protection

Tuvalu lacks specific consumer protection laws. However, in the context of sales of goods, consumers enjoy some limited protection under the Sale of Goods Act (Cap. 40.60), which imposes certain conditions and warranties. There are also product-specific laws of relevance, such as the Food Safety Act 2006 which regulates misleading or deceptive conduct in relation to food (Section 11).

3. Data protection and privacy

The laws of Tuvalu do not specifically address data protection and privacy. Section 21 of the Constitution of Tuvalu does provide some protection for privacy, but it is limited to the traditional contexts of person, home and property, rather than to any notion of protecting personal data.

4. Cybercrime and cybersecurity

In terms of online security, cybercrime and speech-related offences, the Tuvalu Telecommunications Corporation Act (Cap. 35.05) addresses various offences including: intentionally modifying or interfering with the content of a message sent by means of a telecommunication system (s. 33(d)); intentionally intercepting a message sent by means of a telecommunication system (s. 33(e)); intentionally disclosing

196 See https://dfa.gov.tv/index.php/2022/12/12/the-constitution-of-tuvalu-bill-2022/.

197 Online legal information resources seem incomplete: https://tuvalu-legislation.tv/cms/; http://www.paclii.org/countries/tv.html; https://tuvalu.tradeportal.org/Laws?l=en.

198 See https://treaties.un.org/Pages/ViewDetails.aspx?src=TREATY&mtdsg_no=X-20&chapter=10&clang=_en.

the content of a message intercepted in accordance with paragraph (e) above (s. 33(f)); damaging, removing, tampering with, touching or interfering with any telecommunication apparatus or telecommunication line being part of or used in or about any telecommunication system (s. 33(g)); impeding or delaying the correct transmission or the delivery of any message through drunkenness, carelessness or other misconduct (s. 33(j)); and, with intent to deceive, forging or altering a message (s. 33(l)). The Counter Terrorism and Transnational Organised Crime Act 2009 and the Mutual Assistance in Criminal Matters Act 2008 are also relevant in this context.

Beyond this, the Tuvalu legal framework does not encompass specific cybersecurity regulations. Tuvalu is a member of the Pacific Islands Law Officers' Network.[199]

Tuvalu has drafted a Cybercrime Bill but approval is still pending.

5. Intellectual property and copyright

The intellectual property and copyright laws of Tuvalu do not specifically focus on the online environment. The most important instruments –all seemingly technology-neutral– include the Copyright Act (Cap. 40.24), Registration of United Kingdom Patents Act (Cap. 40.48), United Kingdom Designs Protection Act (Cap. 40.68) and Registration of United Kingdom Trade Marks Act (Cap. 40.52). Tuvalu has acceded to the Berne Convention for the Protection of Literary and Artistic Works.

6. Online content regulation

Freedom of expression is established under the Constitution (s. 24). Other Constitutionally guaranteed rights of relevance online include the protection of the law (s. 22), the freedom of belief (s. 23), as well as the freedom of assembly and association (s. 25) and the right of freedom from discrimination (s. 27).

The technology-neutral Penal Code (Cap. 10.20) contains several speech-related offences of relevance for online content regulation. For example, any person who "maliciously fabricates or knowingly spreads abroad or publishes, whether by writing or by word of mouth or otherwise, any false news or false report tending to create or foster public alarm, public anxiety or disaffection or to produce public detriment" shall be guilty of a misdemeanour (s. 60(a)). Further, Part IX addresses sedition and Part XIX addresses defamation.

In addition, the Tuvalu Telecommunications Corporation Act (Cap. 35.05) contains several relevant offences, including "sending, by means of a telecommunication system, a message or other matter that is grossly offensive or of an indecent, obscene or menacing character" (s. 33(b)), or "sending, by such means, a message that that person knows to be false, for the purpose of causing annoyance, inconvenience or needless anxiety to another" (s. 33(c)).

Other general Acts containing speech restrictions specifically refer to electronic communications. For example, in defining the term "publish", the Tobacco Control Act (Cap. 28.14) includes both to "include in any disk for use with a computer" and to "disseminate by means of any other electronic medium" (Sections 3 (f) and 3(g) respectively).

Finally, there are several examples of technology-neutral laws that may impact what content may be displayed online in Tuvalu. For example, Section 17 of the Pharmacy and Therapeutic Products Act 2016 regulates the advertisement of therapeutic products in Tuvalu.

199 See https://pilonsec.org/about/members/.

7. Domain names

The country code top-level domain for Tuvalu is ".tv". In December 2022, it was announced that, under an agreement between the Government of Tuvalu and the GoDaddy company, marketing, sales, promotion and branding of the .tv domain has been outsourced to a newly established .tv unit at the Tuvalu Telecommunications Corporation.[200]

8. Online dispute resolution

Tuvalu has taken steps to encourage dispute resolution outside the court system, for example in the form of the Arbitration Act (Cap. 7.04). Furthermore, an important step in ensuring access to justice was taken in the form of the Small Claims Act (Cap. 7.60) that addresses "personal suit brought in or transferred to a magistrate's court where the value of the property, debt or damage claimed, whether as balance of account or otherwise, is not more than $1,000"[201] (Section 2). However, Tuvalu lacks specific online dispute resolution rules.

9. Digital ID

The laws of Tuvalu do not specifically address digital ID.

10. E-payments

The laws of Tuvalu do not specifically address e-payment.

11. Taxation

The laws of Tuvalu do not specifically address taxation of e-commerce. Important legislation includes the Consumption Tax Act 2008, the Sales Tax Act (Cap. 26.32), and the Income Tax Act 2008. Foreign companies may wish to note Part IX of the International Companies Act 2009, which outlines tax exemptions and specific provisions for international businesses operating in Tuvalu. Tuvalu is a member of the Pacific Islands Tax Administrators Association (PITAA).[202]

200 See https://dfa.gov.tv/index.php/2022/12/13/tv-unit-at-tuvalu-telecommunications-corporation/.
201 Australian dollars.
202 See https://pitaa.org/.

O. Vanuatu

Vanuatu operates under a blended legal system that integrates British, French and customary laws. Its legal foundation includes the Constitution, common law, Vanuatu legislation, case law, as well as statutes and joint regulations inherited from British and French administrations at Independence, alongside Vanuatu customary law.[203]

The National Information and Communication Technology Policy underscores the Government's dedication to maximizing the impact of ICT to realize the national vision of "a just, educated, healthy and wealthy Vanuatu," thereby empowering all citizens and residents. This policy document aims to coordinate efforts among stakeholders effectively. Key priorities include enhancing ICT access in education, infrastructure, and devices; advancing e-government services; integrating ICT into sectoral policies; ensuring cybersecurity and trust; promoting locally relevant content; facilitating capacity building; and fostering multi-stakeholder collaboration and coordination across sectors.

The Vanuatu E-commerce Strategy and Roadmap represents a pivotal initiative and was accelerated by the increased digital readiness of Vanuatu consumers and businesses during the COVID-19 pandemic. It focuses predominantly on enhancing business-to-consumer (B2C) and business-to-business (B2B) models and aligns closely with the Pacific Regional E-commerce Strategy (2021–2025) and the Vanuatu National Sustainable Development Plan (Vanuatu, 2030).

The strategy, under Priority Area 4: Legal and Regulatory Framework, highlights the need for all e-commerce-related laws to be fully based on relevant articles of the UNCITRAL Model Law and aligned with best international practices. It also emphasizes the importance of effectively enforcing the e-commerce regulatory and legal framework and ensuring that policymakers are adequately trained to negotiate bilateral and free trade agreements containing e-commerce provisions.

Legal and regulatory frameworks in Vanuatu require substantial updates to meet the demands of the e-commerce environment. Priority areas for reform include implementing regulations for certification authorities, developing comprehensive e-commerce transaction legislation, ensuring the regulation of a national payment system, and introducing a unified digital identity system. In addition, Vanuatu lacks consumer protection legislation or specific data privacy legislation, both of which are critical for fostering consumer trust in digital platforms. Efforts to strengthen cybersecurity are necessary to safeguard both businesses and consumers engaging in e-commerce.

1. E-transactions /E-signatures

The Electronic Transactions Act 2000 provides a comprehensive regulation of e-transactions (Parts 2 and 3), as well as e-signatures (Part 4).[204] This Act is influenced by the UNCITRAL Model Law on Electronic Commerce (1996).[205] In addition, Vanuatu has a specific E-Business Act (Cap. 264).

203 Online legal information resources seem incomplete: http://www.paclii.org/countries/vu.html; https://www.lexadin.nl/wlg/legis/nofr/oeur/lxwevan.htm;https://parliament.gov.vu/index.php/icons/legislation; https://parliament.gov.vu/index.php/icons/members-of-10th-legislature.

204 See E-commerce in Vanuatu: (paclii.org)

205 See https://uncitral.un.org/en/texts/ecommerce/modellaw/electronic_commerce/status.

2. Consumer protection

Vanuatu lacks general consumer protection legislation. However, there are some provisions within certain sector-specific laws. The Telecommunications and Radiocommunications (Consumer Protection) Regulations Order No.157 of 2015 provides a degree of consumer protection within its specific context, which is regulating matters such as the need to provide accurate and current information about the services (Section 6); the terms of service (s. 4); notification (s. 3); and some forms of advertising practices (s. 10). Finally, Vanuatu is a founding member of the Pacific Island Network of Competition Consumer and Economic Regulators (PINCCER).[206]

3. Data protection and privacy

The right to privacy is emphasized in the Constitution (Section 5(j)). Further, under Section 25 of the Electronic Transactions Act 2000, the Minister responsible for telecommunications and electronic commerce may make orders prescribing standards for the processing of personal data, whether or not the personal data originates inside Vanuatu. The Right to Information Act 2016 provides a definition of "personal information" (s. 3) and includes aspects of a right commonly included in data privacy laws, namely the right to access to information held by public authorities (ss. 8 and 9). Cyber stalking is regulated in Section 10 of the Cybercrime Act No 22 of 2021. Finally, Part 5 of the Telecommunications and Radiocommunications (Consumer Protection) Regulations Order No. 157 of 2015 provides some safeguards for how "consumer information" may be handled. Work on a specific data privacy law is underway[207] and a Bill for the Data Protection and Privacy Act No. of 2024 is under development.

4. Cybercrime and cybersecurity

The Parliament of Vanuatu passed the Cybercrime Act No 22 of 2021.[208] The Act was developed with support from the Council of Europe, in compliance with the Budapest Convention.[209] Part 2 addresses a selection of computer offences, such as illegal access (s. 3) and misuse of devices (s. 6). Part 3 governs computer-related offences including some content-related offences discussed below in the context of online content regulation. The Act also addresses procedural matters (Part 4) and international cooperation (Part 5). In addition, Part 10 of the Telecommunications Act (Cap 206) outlines a range of cyber offences. The Police Powers Act 2017 provides police with certain investigative powers of particular relevance for the cyber environment.

Some of the offences outlined in the Penal Code –with its extraterritorial reach (ss. 2, 4 and 5)– are of special relevance online. Here we may consider seditious statements (s. 65), criminal defamation (s. 120), and obscene publications (s. 140). In addition, some sections specifically refer to the cyber context. For example, Section 147B criminalizes the publishing of child pornography and specifically mentions dissemination via "Internet website"; the definition of a terrorist act includes an act or omission that "is designed or intended to disrupt any computer system or the provision of services directly related to communications infrastructure, banking, financial services, utilities, transportation or other essential infrastructure" (s. 73C(1)(vii)).

206 See https://www.mted.gov.to/index.php/2023/11/07/press-release/.

207 See https://www.coe.int/en/web/data-protection/-/vanuatu-engaged-in-work-on-data-protection-legislation.

208 See https://ogcio.gov.vu/images/Docs/legislation/Cybercrime_Act_n_of_2021.pdf.

209 See https://www.coe.int/en/web/octopus/-/vanuatu?redirect=https://www.coe.int/en/web/octopus/country-wiki?p_p_id=101_INSTANCE_AZnxfNT8Y3ZI&p_p_lifecycle=0&p_p_state=normal&p_p_mode=view&p_p_col_id=column-4&p_p_col_pos=1&p_p_col_count=2.

Regarding cybersecurity, Section 24 of the Electronic Transactions Act 2000 provides the Minister with the power to make regulations in relation to the use, import and export of encryption programmes or products; although no such regulations have been issued to date. The Mutual Assistance in Criminal Matters No. 14 of 2002 may also be noted here. Vanuatu is a member of the Pacific Islands Law Officers' Network.[210]

5. Intellectual property and copyright

For matters of intellectual property and copyright, the primary Acts include the Copyright and Related Rights Act 2000, the Registration of the United Kingdom Trade Marks Act (Cap 81), Registration of United kingdom Patent Act (Cap 80), and the Patents Act 2003 as amended.

Vanuatu has ratified the Berne Convention for the Protection of Literary and Artistic Works, and the Convention Establishing the World Intellectual Property Organization through the Berne Convention for the Protection of Literary and Artistic Works (Ratification) Act 2012, and the Convention Establishing the World Intellectual Property Organization (Ratification) Act 2012, respectively.

6. Online content regulation

Freedom of speech and expression is established under the Constitution (s. 5(g)). Other Constitutionally guaranteed rights of particular relevance online include the right to freedom of conscience and worship (s. 5(f)), as well as the freedom of assembly and association (s. 5(h)) and the right to the protection of the law (s. 5(d)).

The Cybercrime Act No 22 of 2021 governs several content-related offences, including child pornography (ss. 7–8), cyber stalking (s. 10), and computer-related forgery (s. 12).

Some Acts, such as the Obscenity Act, appear technology-neutral and may apply in an online context even though they may pre-date widespread online publication. Similarly, Section 13 of the Public Order Act makes spreading false rumours an offence.

Several Acts now specifically address online content regulation in a sector-specific manner. For example, the Sale of Medicines (Control) (Amendment) Act 2014 makes clear that "A person who intends to sell medicine in Vanuatu via the Internet, must obtain the prior written approval of the Pharmacists Practitioners Commission." (Section 2(2)).

Finally, some Acts –such as the Vanuatu Interactive Gaming Act– were specifically designed with the online environment in mind.

Of relevance for the regulation of online content, Part 6 of the Electronic Transactions Act 2000 regulates the liability of intermediaries and e-commerce service providers.

A Bill for the Harmful Digital Communication Act No. of 2023 and a Bill for the Digital Safety Authority Act No. of 2023 were withdrawn in 2023.

7. Domain names

The country code top-level domain for Vanuatu is ".vu". Since 2019, Neustar Vanuatu Limited (a subsidiary of Neustar, Inc.) is the registry.[211]

8. Online dispute resolution

The laws of Vanuatu do not specifically address online dispute resolution.

210 See https://pilonsec.org/about/members/.

211 See https://www.hello.vu/trbr-appoints-neustar-as-new-back-end-registry-operator-for-vu-country-code-top-level-domain/.

9. Digital ID

The laws of Vanuatu do not specifically address digital ID.

10. E-payments

The laws of Vanuatu do not specifically address e-payment.

11. Taxation

The laws of Vanuatu do not specifically address taxation of e-commerce. Important legislation includes the Tax Administration Act 2018, the International Tax Cooperation Act 2016, and the Value Added Tax Act (Cap 247).

Vanuatu is a member of the Pacific Islands Tax Administrators Association (PITAA).[212]

212 See https://pitaa.org/.

References

APEC (2005). APEC Privacy Framework. Asia–Pacific Economic Cooperation. Singapore. Available at: https://www.apec.org/publications/2005/12/apec-privacy-framework

APEC (2017). *Collaborative Framework for Online Dispute Resolution of Cross-Border Business-to-Business Disputes*. Asia–Pacific Economic Cooperation. Singapore. Available at: https://mddb.apec.org//Documents/2019/EC/EC2/19_ec2_022.pdf

Council of Europe (1981). Convention for the Protection of Individuals with regard to Automatic Processing of Personal Data (Convention 108+). Council of Europe. Strasbourg. Available at: https://www.coe.int/en/web/data-protection/convention108-and-protocol

Council of Europe (2001). Convention on Cybercrime (Budapest Convention). Council of Europe. Strasbourg. Available at: https://www.coe.int/en/web/cybercrime/the-budapest-convention

Commonwealth Secretariat (2023). Model Provisions on Data Protection. Commonwealth Secretariat. London. Available at: https://production-new-commonwealth-files.s3.eu-west-2.amazonaws.com/s3fs-public/2023-02/ROL%20Model%20Law%20Provisions%20on%20Data%20Protection.pdf?VersionId=Fpgmtvhd6E3dm3JfQiEVp8lP0zO_mGy0

Commonwealth Secretariat (2023). Model Law on Computer and Computer-related Crime. Commonwealth Secretariat. London. Available at: https://production-new-commonwealth-files.s3.eu-west-2.amazonaws.com/migrated/key_reform_pdfs/P15370_11_ROL_Model_Law_Computer_Related_Crime.pdf

OECD (2016). Online Dispute Resolution Framework (OECD ODR Framework). Organisation for Economic Co-operation and Development. Paris. Available at: https://www.oecd.org/en/publications/oecd-online-dispute-resolution-framework_325e6edc-en.html#:~:text=The%20framework%20aims%20to%20assist,to%20ensure%20fairness%20and%20transparency.

OECD (2023). Recommendation on of the Council on the Governance of Digital Identity. Organisation for Economic Co-operation and Development. Paris. Available at: https://legalinstruments.oecd.org/en/instruments/OECD-LEGAL-0491#

UNCDF (2023a). *Assessing Digital and Financial Literacy in Timor-Leste: A Survey on Knowledge, Skills and Access.* United Nations Capital Development Fund. Suva. https://www.uncdf.org/article/8606/assessing-digital-and-financial-literacy-in-timor-leste-a-survey-on-knowledge-skills-and-access

UNCDF (2023b). *Assessing Digital and Financial Literacy in Fiji: A Survey on Knowledge, Skills and Access.* United Nations Capital Development Fund. Suva. Available at: https://www.uncdf.org/article/8317/assessing-digital-and-financial-literacy-in-fiji-a-survey-on-knowledge-skills-and-access

UNCDF (2023c). *Assessing Digital and Financial Literacy in Solomon Islands: Survey on Knowledge, Skills and Access*. United Nations Capital Development Fund. Suva. Available at: https://www.uncdf.org/article/8476/assessing-digital-and-financial-literacy-in-solomon-islands

UNCDF (2023d). *Assessing Digital and Financial Literacy in Samoa: A Survey on Knowledge, Skills and Access.* United Nations Capital Development Fund. Suva. Available at: https://www.uncdf.org/article/8489/assessing-digital-and-financial-literacy-in-samoa

UNCDF (2023e). *Assessing Digital and Financial Literacy in Tonga: A Survey on Knowledge, Skills and Access.* United Nations Capital Development Fund. Suva. Available at: https://www.uncdf.org/article/8578/assessing-digital-and-financial-literacy-in-tonga-a-survey-on-knowledge-skills-and-access

UNCDF (2023f). *Assessing Digital and Financial Literacy in Vanuatu: Survey on Knowledge, Skills and Access.* United Nations Capital Development Fund. Suva. Available at: https://www.uncdf.org/article/8607/assessing-digital-and-financial-literacy-in-vanuatu-survey-on-knowledge-skills-and-access

UNCDF (2023g). *Assessing Digital and Financial Literacy in Papua New Guinea: Survey on Knowledge, Skills and Access.* United Nations Capital Development Fund. Suva. Available at: https://www.uncdf.org/article/8648/assessing-digital-and-financial-literacy-in-papua-new-guinea-survey-on-knowledge-skills-and-access

UNCITRAL (2001). Model Law on Electronic Signatures. United Nations Commission on International Trade Law. New York. Available at: https://uncitral.un.org/en/texts/ecommerce/modellaw/electronic_signatures

UNCITRAL (2005). Convention on the Use of Electronic Communications in International Contracts. United Nations Commission on International Trade Law. New York. Available at: https://uncitral.un.org/en/texts/ecommerce/conventions/electronic_communications

UNCITRAL (2013). Procedural Rules for Online Dispute Resolution, Working Group III. United Nations Commission on International Trade Law. New York. Available at: https://uncitral.un.org/en/working_groups/3/online_dispute_resolution

UNCITRAL (2016). Technical Notes on Online Dispute Resolution. United Nations Commission on International Trade Law. New York. Available at: https://uncitral.un.org/sites/uncitral.un.org/files/media-documents/uncitral/en/v1700382_english_technical_notes_on_odr.pdf

UNCITRAL (2017). Model Law on Electronic Transferable Records. United Nations Commission on International Trade Law. New York. Available at: https://uncitral.un.org/en/texts/ecommerce/modellaw/electronic_transferable_records

UNCITRAL (2022). Model Law on the Use and Cross-border Recognition of Identity Management and Trust Services. United Nations Commission on International Trade Law. New York. Available at: https://uncitral.un.org/en/mlit

United Nations (2024). United Nations Convention against Cybercrime. United Nations General Assembly. New York. Available at: https://www.unodc.org/unodc/en/frontpage/2024/August/united-nations_-member-states-finalize-a-new-cybercrime-convention.html

UNCTAD (2025) *Digital Economy Report: Pacific Edition 2024. Available at https://unctad.org/system/files/official-document/dtlecdc2025d1_en.pdf.*

UNCTAD (2025) Indirect Taxation of E-Commerce and Digital Trade: Implications for Developing Countries. Available at https://unctad.org/system/files/official-document/dtlecde2024d2_en.pdf.